The Freshwater Angler™ 2-02

Catching
CATFISH

By Keith Sutton

The Ultimate Guide
• Blues • Flatheads • Channels •

CREATIVE
PUBLISHING
international

MINNETONKA, MINNESOTA

CREDITS

Creative Publishing international, Inc.
5900 Green Oak Drive
Minnetonka, MN 55343
1-800-328-3895

President/CEO: David D. Murphy
Vice President/Editorial: Patricia K. Jacobsen
Vice President/Retail Sales & Marketing: Richard M. Miller

CATCHING CATFISH
By Keith B. Sutton

Executive Editor, Outdoor Group: Don Oster
Editorial Director: David R. Maas
Senior Editor: David L. Tieszen
Managing Editor: Jill Anderson
Creative Director: Brad Springer
Senior Art Director: Dave Schelitzche
Mac Designer: Joe Fahey
Photo Researcher: Angie Hartwell
Director, Production Services: Kim Gerber
Production Staff: Laura Hokkanen, Kay Swanson

Contributing Photographers: (T=Top, B=Bottom, C=Center, L=Left, R=Right, I=Inset)
In-Fisherman—Brainerd, Minnesota
  © In-Fisherman: cover TR
Bill Linder Photography—St. Paul, Minnesota
  © Bill Linder Photography: cover TL, pp. 6-7, 8-9, 24, 30-31
Randie R. Little, Ph. D.—Columbia, Missouri
  © Randie R. Little, Ph. D.: p. 14
John G. New—Chicago, Illinois
  © John G. New: p. 17
Contributing Illustrator:
Joseph R. Tomelleri—Leawood, Kansas
  © Joseph R. Tomelleri: pp. 18, 22, 28-29, 39, 40, 41

Printed on American paper by: R. R. Donnelley & Sons Co.
10 9 8 7 6 5 4 3 2 1

Library of Congress Cataloging-in-Publication Data

Catching catfish: the ultimate guide: blues, flatheads, channels.
    p.cm. -- (Freshwater angler)
  ISBN 0-86573-115-2 (softcover)
    1. Catfishing. I. Creative Publishing International. II. Hunting & Fishing library.
Freshwater angler.
  SH691.C35 C38 2000
  799.1'749--dc21   99-052586

CONTENTS

INTRODUCTION 4

1. UNDERSTANDING CATFISH 6
   Catfish Basics 8
   Catfish Senses 12
   Channel Catfish 18
   Blue Catfish 22
   Flathead Catfish 28
   White Catfish 34
   Bullheads 38
   Other Catfish 42

2. WHERE TO FIND CATFISH 46
   Typical Catfish Waters 48
   Small to Mid-Size Rivers 50
   Big Rivers 56
   Man-Made Lakes 64
   Oxbow Lakes 68
   Ponds 72

3. EQUIPMENT FOR CATCHING CATFISH 76
   Rods, Reels & Line 78
   Terminal Tackle 83
   Catfishing Rigs 90
   Accessories 98
   Natural Baits 103
   Commercial Baits 112

4. CATFISHING TECHNIQUES 118
   Still-Fishing 120
   Drift-Fishing 128
   Trotlining 136
   Jug Fishing 144
   Limblining 148
   Noodling 152

5. SPECIAL SITUATIONS 156
   Thick Cover 158
   Fluctuating Water Levels 162
   Clear Water 165
   Cold Water 168
   Deep Water 171
   Trophy Cats 175
   Catfish Conservation 180
   Cleaning Catfish 184
   Cooking Tips & Recipes 187

INDEX 190

INTRODUCTION

FOR ME AND FOR SO MANY OTHER ANGLERS IN NORTH AMERICA, CATFISH AND THE PLACES THEY RESIDE MAKE US SMILE, AND WE ARE DRAWN TO THE FISH AND TO THOSE PLACES WITH A LONGING THAT IS LIFE CHANGING AND, EVENTUALLY, LIFE DEFINING. MANY OF US ARE WHO WE ARE IN PART BECAUSE WE ARE PASSIONATE ABOUT CATFISH. WE COULD NO MORE FORSAKE CATFISHING THAN SKIP A SEASON OF THE YEAR. AND WE SPEND COUNTLESS HOURS IN DIRECT AND INDIRECT PURSUIT OF THE FISH AND THE REMAINING WILDERNESS WHERE THEY'RE FOUND.

This book is important because it marks history that catfish anglers have long hoped for. While other books about catfishing have been written, none are so comprehensive in their coverage and so impressive in their illustration of this topic of concern to almost 10 million catfish anglers. This marks history, because even 10 years ago the production of a book such as this would have been unthinkable, for until recently, most of the fishing world still considered catfish and catfish anglers a nonentity in fishing. Catfishing has come of age for the first time in the long history of fishing.

So long overdue, when one realizes that catfish are, as much as any group of fish, the fish of the present and the future. Channel catfish, in particular, are as adaptable and therefore widespread as almost any other fish in fresh water. And they grow large and fight hard, besides being superb table fare. Flathead catfish and blue catfish also are widely available, but it is their availability in combination with their awesome size potential that compels anglers today, and, I suggest, will excite even more anglers in the future. These are some of the most impressive fish in fresh water. Sportfish supreme. Big gamefish, I like to say. And, again, they're readily available and not heavily overfished, as is the case with so many other popular sportfish species in North America.

This book is a comprehensive look at the world of catfish and is impressive in its coverage of catfishing. The basis for fine fishing rests first with understanding the biology of each catfish species. Naturally, then, the book begins there, covering the nature of each beast. These chapters are followed by sturdy instruction in where-to and how-to – illustration and explanation of stream, river, reservoir and pond makeup, along with illustrations of rigs and tackle and an explanation of the techniques required to use them. Note, too, the instruction for cleaning and suggestions for cooking these delicious fish, as well as compelling suggestions about conserving catfish for today and tomorrow.

In the end, though, this book leads full circle, back to why we fish for these whiskered creatures. It's the wilderness in which these catfish reside. It's the lifelong friendships that develop alongside the pursuit. It's the ever-changing challenge of the pursuit. And it's how well catfish adapt to any common man's table fare, served so easily in a dozen ways. No wonder so many anglers fish for catfish with a passion that reaches beyond common sense.

Doug Stange, Editor-in-Chief
In-Fisherman *magazine*

UNDERSTANDING
CATFISH

Catfish Basics

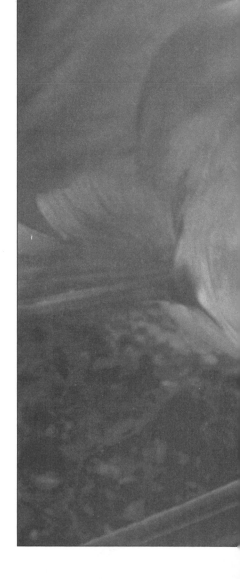

What makes a fish a catfish? Well, first of all, it must have whiskers, or correctly, *barbels*. After all, that's where the catfish got its name. These paired appendages remind some folks of the whiskers on our furry house pets. All North American catfish possess four pairs of barbels around the mouth. The barbels are organs of taste and feel. They're sensitive to touch and covered with taste buds. Thus, they assist a catfish in finding food, even in muddy water. Some folks think the barbels can sting, but this is only a myth.

Catfish have sharp spines in their pectoral and dorsal fins. Unlike barbels, these can inflict painful wounds. Many "cats" have venom cells in the skin covering these spines.

All catfish lack scales. There are those with smooth, naked skins (like our native cats), others with rows of spiny plates and even a few completely armored with overlapping shields. But no scales. They also possess a fleshy adipose fin on the rear of their back, like trout and salmon.

More than 2,200 species of catfish swim the waters of the world (about 8 percent of the total number of fishes). They're found on every continent except Antarctica and comprise what many fish scientists consider the most diverse group of fish on earth. There are bigger fish and littler fish, stranger fish, more beautiful fish and even uglier fish. But in no other group of fish does so much beauty and ugliness come together.

On the ugly end of the scale is the wels, or sheatfish, the giant cat of Eurasian rivers and lakes. Individuals nearly 15 feet long and some weighing more than 600 pounds have been reported. Stories of children being swallowed whole by these fish are part of European folklore. They are said to devour birds and dogs swimming at the surface.

The giant Mekong catfish, or pla buek, of Southeast Asia is another behemoth. It grows to 12 feet and 650 pounds. The goonah of India, a hulking catfish with a massive jaw, grows to 5 feet and weighs almost as much as a man.

At least three South American cats – the redtailed cat, jau and azulejo – have been documented at weights over 200 pounds. They grow heavier, but big ones just can't be caught. The vundu and sharptooth cats of Africa exceed 65 pounds.

Among the more beautiful catfish are the many species of Corydoras and plecos popular with home aquarists. Many are brightly colored or covered with intricate designs of spots, speckles and stripes.

The catfish family includes many unusual members as well. Africa's electric catfish, an aggressive animal that may weigh more than 50 pounds, packs a punch of up to 300 volts, enough to run a hair dryer.

The upside-down catfish is another African native. This little backswimmer starts out with the conventional dark back and light belly but takes to swimming upside down as it grows and ends up with a light-colored back and a dark-colored belly.

The Asian glass catfish is transparent. If you look at one through a magnifying glass, you can see its heart beating. Should one die, it immediately turns milky white, a fact that suggests it does something while alive to maintain its transparency.

The talking catfish of South America are also aptly named. These fish emit a high-pitched croaking noise, which can be surprisingly loud. The fish accomplishes this by grinding the base of its pectoral fin bone against its shoulder bone. Most, if not all, of the 80 to 100 species in this genus can "talk" in this manner. Amongst these are some true giants (4 feet plus), which must be eerie to hear.

The most fearsome reputation belongs not to one of the giant catfish but to tiny South American cats called candirus. These 1/2-inch-long blood-sucking, eel-like cats have the unique distinction of being the only vertebrates that parasitize humans. They have the peculiar, and frightening, habit of entering the human genital opening, of either male or female, and worming their way up into the urethra, where they erect prickly spines on their gill covers, embedding themselves within the body of their human host. Many victims die in agony.

North America north of Mexico is home to 45 catfish species, quite a meager collection compared to other continents. But what we lack in quantity, we make up in quality. The "big three" of North American catfish – blue, flathead and channel – rank among the world's largest. Learn more about them in the following sections of this book.

Catfish Senses

When it comes to senses, catfish are turbo-charged. Their sense of taste is unbelievable. Their sense of smell is unparalleled. Few fish hear as well, and catfish also have excellent sight and a superb sense of touch. On top of all that, catfish have other sensory abilities that seem more like science fiction than science fact. To say the least, they are highly attuned to the world around them.

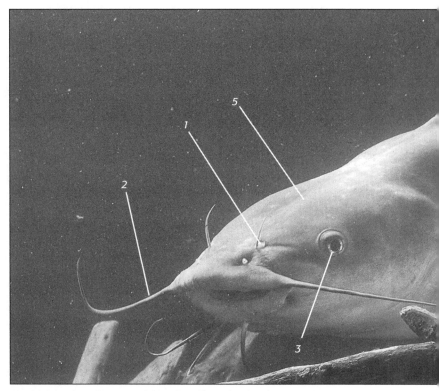

CATFISH are literally covered from head to tail with sensory organs. The photo above shows the location of their external sensory organs. The nostrils (1) lead to the complex olfactory pits. The barbels (2) and most of the body are covered with taste buds. The back of the eyes (3) are coated

SMELL. Catfish smell real good. Well, they don't really smell good, but they have an extraordinary sense of smell. Their smellers are right up front, in two little pits located in front of the eyes and behind the upper jaw.

With this keen sense of smell they can detect food at long distances, but also in water where visibility may only be a few inches. Each olfactory pit has two nostrils, one for incoming water and one for outgoing water. These pits are lined with sensitive tissue wrinkled into a series of folds (right) to provide the maximum surface area for

Nasal folds of a channel catfish's olfactory pit

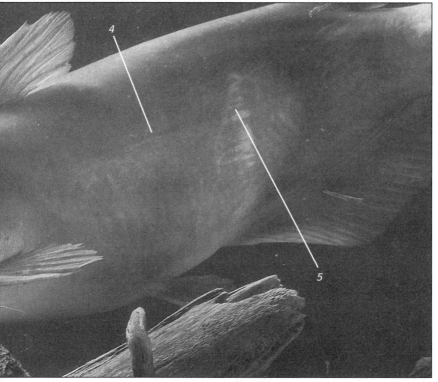

with a layer of crystals that reflect light. The lateral line (4) detects vibrations in the water. Electroreceptive pores (5) cover the head region and the lateral line.

smelling. The number of these folds is related to sharpness of smell. Channel cats have more than 140. Rainbow trout have only 18, largemouth bass 8 to 13.

Water is drawn into one nostril, over the sensory tissue and out the other nostril. Catfish detect some compounds at one part per 10 billion parts of water. If a substance is determined to be a potential food item, a message is sent to the brain telling the catfish to move toward the object for further investigation.

TASTE. The catfish's highly developed sense of taste is like something out of *Ripley's Believe It or Not*. The smooth, scaleless skin is completely covered with taste buds. A catfish just 6 inches long has more than a quarter million. On a giant blue cat or flathead . . . well, who knows. No one wants to count them.

Imagine a huge swimming tongue. In a way, that's what a catfish is.

Most fishes' taste buds are only found in the mouth – on the tongue, the palate and so forth. There aren't that many of them, either. In catfish, the mouth is packed with dense concentrations of taste buds. The major flow of water is across the gills, so gill rakers facing water flow also are loaded with huge densities of taste buds. Taste buds are also found on the outside of catfish as well – their fins, their back, their belly, their sides, even their tail.

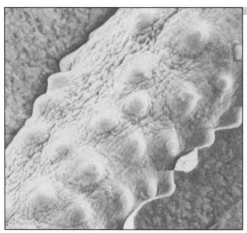

A CATFISH'S WHISKERS are covered with thousands of taste buds, which look like little "volcanoes" in this microscopic photo.

On the flank of an adult channel or blue cat, there are at least 5,000 taste buds per square centimeter of skin. The highest concentrations on the outside of the body, however, are on the whiskers. Look at a catfish whisker under a microscope, and you'll see what resembles a field of volcanoes. Every volcano is a taste bud.

The taste buds function in two ways. Those covering the body help catfish locate food, even in dark, muddy water. They detect chemicals from nearby food that help the fish close in on the potential morsel. Then, when the cat is near, the long tapered whiskers are used as "feelers" to cautiously sample the food. If everything's kosher so far, the catfish mouths the item. Taste buds in the mouth then determine whether the food item is edible.

HEARING. Catfish don't have ears, right? No, that's not right. They don't have ears we can see, but they don't need them. They "hear" by receiving sound waves through their skin.

Actually, a catfish's ear is its swim bladder. That's part of it, anyway. The swim bladder contains gas, creating an air space with a different density from the rest of the fish. When sound waves hit the bladder, it vibrates, just like our eardrums. This amplifies the sound waves, which then travel to small ear bones called *otoliths* in the inner ear. The otoliths start vibrating, too. As they vibrate, they bend little hair-like projections on the cells beneath them, which transfer a message to the brain.

The swim bladder on most fish is independent of the inner ear. But in catfish, nature built a series of vertebral bones known as the *Weberian apparatus*, connecting the swim bladder and inner ear. Fish without these bone connections (bass and trout, for instance) detect sounds from about 20 to 1,000 cycles per second. The hearing of catfish, however, is much more acute. They hear sounds of much higher frequency, up to about 13,000 cycles per second.

Low-frequency sounds that cannot be detected by the catfish's inner ear are picked up by a series of little pores running along the fish's sides, called the *lateral line*. Similar pores exist around the eye, down the lower jaw and over the head. Inside the pores are cells with little hair-like projections, similar to those in the inner ear. These projections bend in response to water displacement, thus stimulating nerve endings that signal the brain. Catfish use this system to locate nearby prey, potential enemies and members of their own kind. Creatures scurrying across the bottom, flopping at the surface, swimming through the water or walking along a riverbank all create low-frequency vibrations in the water, which the catfish's lateral line detects.

Bullheads in particular are ultra-sensitive to low-frequency vibrations. The Chinese have used them for centuries to warn of earthquakes. Apparently, they can detect rumblings beneath the earth's crust days in advance.

Channel catfish raised in aquaculture ponds also exhibit sensitivity to low-frequency vibrations. They often rise to the surface in response to the footsteps of a person walking over to feed them. This behavior may be noted even when the person is 100 yards or more away!

The lesson here: don't bang around in your boat or stomp around on shore. One way or another, catfish will hear you.

SIGHT. With their beady little eyes, it would seem catfish have poor sight. This is a fallacy. All our catfish have excellent vision. They frequently feed on live fish and use eyesight to capture this fleet prey. In clear waters, sight is probably the primary sense used to zero in on live forage animals.

When you see a deer or raccoon in your headlights at night, their eyes glow from the reflection of light on a thin layer of crystals at the back of the eye, called the *tapetum lucidum*. This structure reflects gathered light back at the retina, greatly aiding night vision. Walleyes are probably the fish most known for having a tapetum. Catfish also have it but to a lesser degree.

Scientists say rods and cones are present in roughly equal numbers in a catfish's eye. Rods allow vision in dim light, and cones offer color vision in daylight.

ELECTROSENSING. Perhaps the most amazing sense possessed by catfish is that of electroreception. Look closely on a catfish's head and you'll notice small scattered pores (opposite page). These are sensory organs that detect electrical fields in living organisms. Electroreceptive pits also are in and along the lateral line. Thanks to these specialized

A MAGNIFIED electroreceptive pore. A catfish's head is covered with thousands of these.

organs, a catfish doesn't have to see its prey or smell it or taste it or feel it; it can find its prey through electroreception, just like sharks.

Every living cell is a battery. That is, if you were to stick an electrode inside a cell and another outside that cell, you would get a reading just as if you were measuring a battery with a voltmeter. Catfish can detect these electrical fields in their prey at very minute levels, the equivalent of detecting a flashlight battery at several thousand yards. With single small forage animals, however, the catfish must be very close – within an inch or less – for this method of detection to work. Work it does, though. This sense is extremely beneficial in dark, muddy water or when cats are digging in mud or sand to find insect larvae and other invertebrates.

The exceptionally powerful senses of catfish enable them to thrive in a wide variety of habitats. They cope better than other fish in difficult environments, and thus are often found where other fish are not. As catman Steve Quinn once put it, "Catfish can where other fish can't." The next time you feel a big catfish tugging on your line, think about how it found your bait. It will help you better appreciate the remarkable senses of these extraordinary fish.

Channel Catfish

(Ictalurus punctatus)

Channel catfish are fish so popular, so well-studied and so varied in their day-to-day activities, they could be the subject of an entire book.

COMMON NAMES. Their nicknames are many. In some areas they are dubbed blue channel, fiddler, speckled cat, spotted cat, blue cat, blue fulton or chucklehead. In other parts of their range, eel cat, willow cat and Great Lakes cat are common tags. These other names are holdovers from a time when channel cats were separated into three different species, all with slightly different physical characteristics. Not until the 1940s were these "species" determined to be simply variations of the plain old channel cat.

DESCRIPTION. Channel cats are the pin-ups of the catfish world – much sleeker and more attractive than flatheads and blues. Most are silvery gray to coppery brown with a white belly. Breeding males are deep blue-black with thickened lips and a knobby, swollen head. The sides of juveniles are peppered with small black spots that fade in adulthood. They have a deeply forked tail and a prominent upper jaw that extends well beyond the lower. Channel cats are sometimes confused with blue catfish. The best way to distinguish between the two is to look at the anal fin. The anal fin of a channel cat has 24 to 29 rays and is rounded. If the fin has a straight outer edge and 30 or more rays, it's a blue cat.

RANGE. Although once confined primarily to the Mississippi River drainage and the Great Lakes, stocking has expanded their range to include every state but Alaska. Channel cats are found from coast to coast, north into four Canadian provinces and south to central Mexico. They are the most widespread and abundant catfish in North America.

Channel Catfish

SIZE. Channels are mid-sized models as catfish go, averaging 1 to 5 pounds. Six- to 10-pounders are common in many waters. The 47.5-inch-long world-record from South Carolina's Lake Moultrie weighed 58 pounds. Only two other states – Arkansas and Mississippi – have produced channel cats over 50 pounds. In most waters, a 20-pounder is a trophy.

AGE & GROWTH. Channel cats more than 20 years old have been recorded, but most live less than 10. They grow slower than both flatheads and blues.

Growth rates have been studied throughout the fish's range and show extreme variability from one body of water to another. A 5-year-old channel cat from the Mississippi River in Iowa, for example, runs about 16 inches long. A same-age fish from Lake Havasu, California, is slightly more than half that length – 9 inches. A 20-inch channel from Manitoba's

Typical Weight (pounds) at Various Lengths (inches)

Length	12	15	18	21	24	27	30	33	36
Weight	.5	1.3	2.7	3.3	5.8	8.8	11.6	15.3	20.4

Typical Length (inches) at Various Ages

Age	1	2	3	4	5	6	7	8	9
North	5.7	7.1	9.0	10.5	12.3	14.1	15.9	18.4	19.7
South	10.9	13.7	15.7	17.8	19.0	21.6	22.6	23.5	24.3

Red River is probably age 9, but a 9-year-old cat from the St. Lawrence River in Quebec is only 13 inches. Growth rates are determined by a number of factors, including abundance and type of forage, quality of habitat, length of the growing season and competition with other fish species.

HABITAT. Channel cats inhabit everything from tiny farm ponds, crystal-clear creeks and sluggish bayous to cypress-shrouded oxbow lakes, vast man-made impoundments and broad lowland rivers. They tolerate a wide variety of environmental conditions, but despite popular misconceptions, do not prefer muddy, poor-quality waters. They fare best in clean, warm, well-oxygenated water with slow to moderate current and abundant cover in the form of logs, boulders, cavities and debris. They are extremely adaptable creatures, and are one of the most stocked gamefish in farm ponds. Their preferred temperature range is between 75° and 80°F.

FOOD HABITS. Channel cats aren't the least bit finicky when it comes to food. Live worms, salamanders, maggots, leeches, caterpillars, insects, frogs, fish, mussels and crayfish are among the creatures they eat. The dead and smelly are also relished – things like shrimp, fish guts, chicken liver and stinkbait. Even bizarre offerings like soap, hot dogs, dog food, corn, marshmallows, grapes, persimmons, elm seeds and bread entice them at times. Adults typically retire to deep water during daylight hours or lie about drift piles, submerged logs and other cover. At night they move into shallower water to feed. Although they can still be caught when water temperatures drop below 50°F, channel cats are less aggressive feeders than blue cats during cold water periods.

REPRODUCTION. Spawning begins when the water temperature is around 75°F – May through July in mid-America. Male channels select and clean a nest site, usually a semi-dark, secluded cavity such as an undercut bank, a hole in a pile of drift logs or perhaps a muskrat or beaver burrow. The female deposits a large mound of golden yellow eggs in the bottom of the nest, then leaves. The male stays, protecting the nest cavity from predators and fanning the eggs to keep them aerated and free from sediments. The eggs hatch in about a week, and the fry remain in the nest for another 7 or 8 days. The male guards the fry until they leave the nest.

The male takes little or no food while spawning, but his protective instinct makes him vulnerable. He strikes any foreign object coming too near the nest cavity, including fishing lures, bait and human hands.

POPULARITY. In popularity polls, channel cats rank high. They are the most popular fish in four states, second most popular in two, and third most popular in nine. No wonder! They readily take a wide variety of baits, and when they're in a feeding mood, it's not unusual to catch several dozen on an outing. They are aggressive fighters and among the tastiest fish on earth. In some regions, they are the only large predator fish available to anglers. Tally up their strong points, and you'll see why channel cats are among the most sought-after fish in the nation.

Channel Catfish Farming

THE DEMAND for channel catfish as a food fish has spawned a multi-million-dollar aquaculture business, with millions of pounds of farm-raised catfish shipped annually to restaurants and grocery stores throughout the U.S. In 1997, 525 million pounds of live-weight catfish were processed, a record for the industry. Prepared catfish products that year totaled 262 million pounds, which translates into 1 pound of catfish consumed per person in the United States. That makes farm-raised catfish the nation's fifth most popular fish. In the primary catfish-producing states of Mississippi, Arkansas, Louisiana and Alabama, the catfish farming industry employs about 13,000 people and contributes more than $4 billion to the individual states' economies. In 1997, direct sales of farm-raised catfish by United States processors were valued at $591 million.

Pond-raised catfish are fed a gourmet diet of puffed, high-protein food pellets (a mix of soybeans, corn, wheat, vitamins and minerals) that allows them to grow much faster than their wild cousins. A 4- to 6-inch farm-raised fingerling reaches $1\frac{1}{2}$ pounds in about 18 months. At this size they are harvested with seines, then taken alive to processing plants in aerated trucks. Once they reach the plants, the whole production process takes less than 30 minutes, making United States farm-raised catfish among the freshest fish available.

Blue Catfish

(Ictalurus furcatus)

I n November 1983, a geologist looking for rock out-
crops near Camden, Arkansas, saw a piece of bone protruding from a dirt embankment. Pulling out the bone,
the man discovered a 2-foot-long skull with a jutting 9-
inch dorsal fin. Paleontologists later identified the specimen as the remains of a 10-foot-long, 1,500-pound catfish
that swam the seas 40 million years ago.

Since the unnamed Camden catfish is now extinct (what a
pity), we are left with the blue cat as one of the giants of
North American catfish.

COMMON NAMES. Monikers include fulton, blue
channel, humpback cat, silver cat, white cat, great blue cat,
highfin blue, white fulton and forktail cat.

DESCRIPTION. Blue catfish vary in color from slate-blue
to grayish brown on their back and sides, fading to a
whitish belly. In muddy waters, some individuals appear
albinistic, the pale skin evoking the common nickname
"white cat." They are often confused with channel catfish.
Both have forked tails and similar coloration, but blues
lack the small black spots punctuating the sides of young
channels, and their anal fin has a straight edge, with 30 or
more fin rays (right).

Trophy-class blues are reminiscent of Japanese sumo wrestlers. Healthy individuals are bizarrely obese, with enormous pot bellies. Small blue cats are streamlined, muscular and often distinctly hump-backed.

RANGE. Blue catfish occur in portions of at least 30 states, from Iowa to southern Texas and from Nebraska to North Carolina. They're also found throughout the eastern third of Mexico and south into Guatemala. The native range encompasses the major rivers

Blue Catfish

A BLUE CATFISH'S ANAL FIN has 30 or more rays and a straighter edge than that of a channel catfish.

of the Mississippi, Ohio and Missouri river basins of the central and southern United States, but blues have also been introduced in Washington, California and Arizona. State fisheries agencies stock millions in large and small impoundments across the country.

In some areas at the fringe of their range – West Virginia, for instance – blue catfish are so rare they're considered a species of special concern. They're also uncommon over much of their northern range, a decline triggered by commercial fishing, dam construction and stream channelization projects. Alterations have mostly removed the combination of swift runs and deep pools blue cats need to flourish.

SIZE. The largest specimen recorded this century weighed 128 pounds. It was caught in the Whiskey Bay Pilot Channel in Louisiana's Atchafalaya Basin in 1978. The world rod-and-reel record is a 112-pounder caught in 1998 from Tennessee's Cumberland River. This broke the previous all-tackle record established by a 111-pound Alabama blue caught in 1996. As a practical matter, a 60-pound blue cat would be the trophy of a lifetime, and the average hook-and-line fish is under 15 pounds.

Blues over 100 pounds were apparently common in the nineteenth century, and there were rare reports of 200- to 300-pound specimens. Blues over 130 pounds haven't been reported in recent years, but the 1990s produced a resurgence in the number of heavyweight blue cats being taken. This decade saw the world record advance from 109 to 112 pounds, plus an unprecedented string of 26 state records, including several blues exceeding 100 pounds.

HABITAT. By nature, blues are big-river fish. They prefer clearer, faster water than other cats, and are usually found over a hard sand or gravel bottom. If you want to catch a heavyweight, don't waste time fishing creeks, ponds or small lakes. Blues are less likely to be found in slow, turbid waters than other catfish, but they are adaptable.

FOOD HABITS. In many respects, the behavior of blue catfish parallels that of striped bass. Like stripers, large blues feed primarily on shad, herring and other schooling baitfish; consequently they are on the move more than other cats and are frequently found in open-water habitat. Blue cats also favor areas of heavy current, while channel cats and flatheads prefer areas with slow to moderate water flow.

Blue cats are active year-round, except when water temperature falls below 40 degrees. Most anglers fish for them during warm months, but many are learning the species' habit of gathering in large feeding schools during winter. Some schools may contain several trophy-class fish. Most hold near the deepest well-oxygenated bottom structure available.

Blue catfish also take crayfish, insects, clams and other invertebrates. Smaller fish are taken on commercial baits, such as stinkbaits and chicken livers, but not as readily as channel catfish.

REPRODUCTION. This species' reproductive habits are poorly known, but thought to be similar to those of channel catfish. Those stocked in reservoirs sometimes grow to enormous sizes, but few, if any, reproduce.

AGE & GROWTH. Despite the massive size documented for this fish, most growth studies show a 10-year-old blue cat measuring only 24 to 36 inches long. Giant blues from such waters must be ancient animals. Under favorable conditions, however, blues exhibit a much greater growth rate.

Typical Length (inches) at Various Ages

Age	1	2	3	4	5	6	7	8	9	10
Length	6.2	11.1	14.7	18.3	22.1	25.5	28.8	30.6	32.3	34.1

Typical Weight (pounds) at Various Lengths (inches)

Length	20	24	28	32	36	40	44	48
Weight	2.9	5.4	9.5	15.3	23.2	33.7	47.3	64.4

POPULARITY. In much of the South and Midwest, blue catfish populations remain healthy, and anglers targeting prime waters have an excellent chance of hooking a trophy fish. In fact, in many rivers and lakes, blue catfish are a largely untapped resource.

They are one of the strongest fighting freshwater fish and considered excellent table fare. In fact, many guides in the South and Southeast specifically target blue cats for their clients. There are few other species that offer a legitimate shot at a 100-pound fish.

On the down side, blue cats are also a favorite of commercial fishermen. On many bodies of water, the commercial harvest remains largely unregulated, and some trophy blue cat populations are slowly disappearing. A few state agencies are starting to implement regulations to reduce the harvest of these monster fish.

Giants of the Past

HISTORICAL RECORDS recount many instances of enormous blues caught from big rivers in the 1800s.

The Missouri River seemed to be a standout among hot spots. A 315-pound blue was supposedly caught near Morrison, Missouri, "just after the Civil War."

According to the Wahoo, Nebraska, New Era in 1892, there was a "monster catfish caught near Bellevue that measured nine feet long," most likely a gigantic blue. Reports of Missouri River catfish heavier than 100 pounds were frequent, and in 1862, news reports recorded many blue cats caught near Yankton, South Dakota, that weighed between 200 and 300 pounds.

Further evidence of the blue catfish's size potential is offered by naturalist Constantine Rafinesque, who in 1820 wrote of catfish, undoubtedly blues, "weighing 185 pounds and another, 250 pounds." P.R. Hoy, a naturalist who traveled across Missouri in 1854, reported that on May 14 of that year, "A lad caught on hook and line today a catfish weighing 136 pounds" from the Grand River near Chillicothe.

The Mississippi River was another mother lode of giant blues. In November 1879, a 150-pound blue catfish taken from the river near St. Louis was sent to the U.S. National Museum by Dr. J.G.W. Steedman, chairman of the Missouri Fish Commission, who found it in a St. Louis fish market. Part of a letter sent by Dr. Steedman to Professor Spencer Baird, U.S. Commissioner of Fish and Fisheries, suggests that catfish of this size were not uncommon: "Your letter requesting the shipment to you of a large Mississippi Catfish was received this morning. Upon visiting our market this P.M. I luckily found two – one of 144 lbs., the other 150 lbs. The latter I ship to you by express."

Even Mark Twain was intrigued with these giants, having seen a "Mississippi catfish that was more than six feet long." It's likely blues near, perhaps over, the 150-pound mark are swimming in some lakes and rivers today. One probably will turn up sometime in the next few years.

Flathead Catfish

(Pylodictis olivaris)

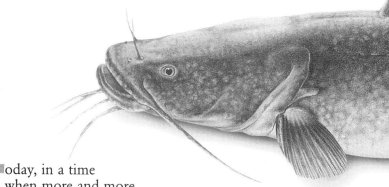

Today, in a time when more and more anglers are seeking greater thrills and bigger fish, the old-time catters are being joined by increasing numbers of fishermen who also seek the flathead. After decades of being overlooked, the flathead is suddenly "in."

COMMON NAMES. Among those commonly heard are yellow cat, shovelhead, mud cat, tabby cat, Morgan cat, appaloosa cat, appaluchion, johnnie cat, goujon, Opelousas cat, Op cat, bashaw, Russian cat, granny cat, pied cat, flatbelly and Mississippi cat.

DESCRIPTION. The flathead catfish is a brute of a fish, muscular and streamlined, but ugly by all accepted standards. The back and sides are brownish to yellowish, with varying degrees of mottling. The belly is a light yellow to creamy white. Its head is broad and flattened, hence its name. Flatheads have a squarish tail and a lower jaw that

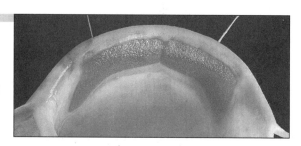

THE TOOTH PAD on the inside upper jaw extends back on both ends.

protrudes beyond the upper. Young fish may be confused with bullheads, but the tooth pad of a flathead extends back into the mouth at each end (opposite page, bottom).

Flathead Catfish

RANGE. Flatheads are widespread, another factor heightening their popularity. They inhabit waters from Minnesota south into Alabama, Texas and Mexico, and east to Pennsylvania and West Virginia. They have also been introduced in many waters west of the Rocky Mountains.

SIZE. Certainly, part of the flathead's appeal stems from its immense size. Five-, ten-, even twenty-pounders are common, and in prime waters, trophy status is granted only to those exceeding 50 or 60 pounds. The world rod-and-reel record from Elk City Reservoir in Kansas stands at 123 pounds, but flatheads nearly 5 feet long weighing almost 140 pounds have been caught commercially in recent times. In the fresh waters of North America, they are exceeded in size only by blue catfish, white sturgeon and alligator gar.

HABITAT. Flatheads are primarily fish of large rivers and impoundments and are seldom found in creeks, ponds and small lakes. Adults live in deep, sluggish pools near submerged logs, piles of driftwood, undercut banks or other cover. They prefer hard sand or gravel bottoms, and are rarely found in areas with a soft bottom. At night, they move from deeper water to shallows to feed. They are solitary fish, and a single spot of cover usually yields only one, at most two or three, adult fish.

FOOD HABITS. Though sometimes taken during daylight hours – especially during overcast or rainy periods or when water is highly colored – flatheads, like all catfish, are primarily nocturnal feeders. Big flatheads scavenge very little and are highly efficient predators, preferring live food, especially fish and crayfish. They rarely are caught using chicken liver, stinkbaits or other dead, malodorous allurements that may tempt blue and channel catfish.

A study conducted in Georgia's Flint River bears this out. Researcher Steve Quinn examined stomach contents of flathead catfish from the river. He found flatheads less than 12 inches long fed primarily on invertebrates, mostly crayfish. Flatheads between 12 and 24 inches subsisted almost entirely on a diet of crayfish. In flatheads greater than 24 inches, the diet was 96 percent fish by weight, primarily gizzard shad, sunfish, suckers and other catfish.

AGE & GROWTH. Flatheads grow fast, adding weight quicker than any other North American gamefish with the possible exception of common carp and grass carp. The fastest growth spurt typically occurs between ages 3 and 8, when they commonly add 2 to 5 pounds per year. Even big flats grow fast, however, with tag returns indicating

Typical Weight (pounds) at Various Lengths (inches)

Length	20	25	30	35	40	45	50
Weight	3.4	6.7	12.1	20.0	30.2	51.3	70.2

Typical Length (inches) at Various Ages

Age	1	2	3	5	7	9	11	13	15
North	7.5	10.9	14.8	19.3	23.9	28.0	35.5	37.0	40.0
South	–	16.3	24.3	27.7	34.7	36.3	40.4	44.2	46.3

increases of more than 10 pounds annually in some cases. In some southern rivers and reservoirs, flatheads have reached 30 pounds in less than 10 years. They are known to live up to 20 years.

REPRODUCTION. Spawning habits are similar to those of the channel cat. Adults excavate a saucer-shaped depression in a natural cavity. Thousands of eggs are laid in a compact yellow mass. The male guards the nest, agitating the eggs by fin movements to keep silt off the eggs and provide oxygen. The young form a tight school for a few days after hatching and then disperse to assume a solitary life. Spawning begins when the water temperature is between 70° and 80°F.

Flatheads have relatively low reproductive potential and are much slower to mature compared to other catfish. A female is usually 4 to 6 years old when mature and produces only about 1,000 eggs per pound of body weight. Channel and blue cats mature in 2 to 3 years and produce 3,000 to 4,000 eggs per pound of body weight.

POPULARITY. Despite its lack of beauty, the flathead draws a passionate cadre of fans. Walk into a bait shop beside prime flathead waters, and you'll see their faded photos tacked to the wall, photos of leathery men grinning and grunting as they strain to hoist a 40-, 50- or 60-pound flat up before the camera, white-knuckled hands gripping the gill plates.

Were you to talk with the fishermen in those photos, they would tell you, in their own words, that flatheads possess an intrinsic mesmerism. Catch one, regardless of the method – on rod-and-reel, a trotline, a limbline or yanked from an underwater hidey-hole with your bare hands – and you become, forevermore, a flathead fan.

Blue-ribbon eating quality is another flathead hallmark. The flesh of even large flatheads is firm, white, flaky and, when properly prepared, absolutely delicious. They support a thriving commercial fishery in parts of the Ohio, Mississippi and Missouri river drainages, and one heavy fish may feed a hungry family for weeks.

Best of all, the flathead catfish is an incomparable fighter. It is a bullish battler, long on sullen anger and short on hysteria.

Flathead Introductions, Bad & Good

THE FLATHEAD'S big mouth and gluttonous appetite sometimes get it in trouble. In some rivers where flatheads have been introduced, they are despised by sunfish anglers who rightfully blame them for declines in redbreast and bluegill populations. Some state fisheries agencies have responded with eradication programs, including legalization of commercial fishing with low-voltage electrofishing rigs. (Catfish fans, on the other hand, often consider flathead predation of sunfish a favorable food conversion.)

In other waters, flatheads are intentionally stocked by fisheries biologists hoping to thin stunted sunfish and bullheads. In Prairie Rose Lake in Iowa, for example, an over-abundant bullhead population had decreased by 60 percent 6 years after flatheads were introduced. As a result, bullheads, which are popular Iowa gamefish, increased in both length and weight, and populations of bluegills and crappie showed improvements in growth and significant increases in numbers.

White Catfish

(Ameiurus catus)

White cats are perhaps the most overlooked and underutilized of our large catfish. Their seeming lack of popularity is not due to scarcity, for these handsome cats are common in numerous waters throughout their range. It's not because white cats aren't sporty opponents, either. They are aggressive, high-spirited scrappers that guarantee hard strikes and rod-bending fights. Inch for inch and pound for pound, they are the equal of any channel cat, flathead or blue.

COMMON NAMES. Fork-tail cat, Potomac cat.

DESCRIPTION. White cats are sort of "in-between" catfish. They have the proportions of a brown bullhead, the silvery blue color of a blue cat and a tail not quite so deeply forked as a channel's. Specimens over 10 pounds intensify the confusion. Their mottled colors and slimmer proportions make them look almost identical to channel cats without spots.

Even scientists have a hard time deciding what they are. At one time white cats were considered more closely related to channel cats than bullheads and were placed in the scientific genus *Ictalurus* with channel cats and blues. Now the opposite is true, and scientists place them in the genus *Ameiurus* with bullheads.

Many fishermen think the white cats they catch are small blues or channels. The best way to tell the trio apart is to

examine the anal fin and the chin barbels. White cats differ from channels and blues in having fewer anal fin rays (19 to 23) and white chin barbels.

RANGE. Before introductions of other species, white catfish were the largest of the native catfishes found in

White Catfish

rivers draining into the Atlantic, from New York's Hudson River southward through Florida. Whites are also native to tributaries of the Gulf of Mexico in Alabama and Mississippi. Their ability to adapt and reproduce in a variety of water conditions makes them appealing to fisheries managers, and they have been transplanted to ponds, lakes and rivers in California, Connecticut, Illinois, Indiana, Kentucky, Massachusetts, Nevada, New Hampshire, Ohio, Oregon and Rhode Island. Healthy populations often are present in brackish water of coastal rivers where other cats are absent.

SIZE. Whites don't grow as big as blue or channel catfish, but 3- to 5-pounders are not uncommon. White cats of 6 pounds and more are exceptional in most waters. The world rod-and-reel record, a truly unusual fish, weighed 22 pounds.

Typical Weight (pounds) at Various Lengths (inches)

Length	8	10	12	14	16	18	20	22
Weight	.17	.35	.64	1.0	1.7	2.3	3.2	4.3

Typical Length (inches) at Various Ages

Age	1	2	3	4	5	6	8	10	12
North	4.6	5.9	7.3	8.3	9.6	10.4	13.3	16.7	20.0
South	4.9	6.6	9.5	12.2	14.9	16.3	18.9	–	–

AGE & GROWTH. Whites grow slowly when compared to other catfish species. In the Santee-Cooper lakes of South Carolina, a 1-year-old fish averages about 5 inches. Fish as old as 14 years have been documented.

REPRODUCTION. Like other members of their family, white cats are nest builders. Both parents help excavate the large nest, usually on sand or gravel bottom near the shore, sometimes protected by logs. The males guard and aerate the eggs and care for the young. Spawning occurs when waters reach about 70 degrees.

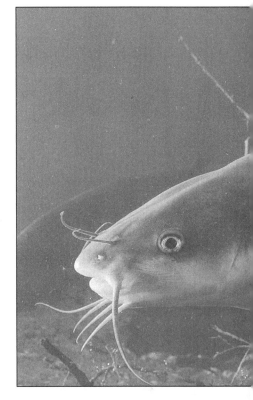

HABITAT. In rivers, the white cat's home area often overlaps that of bullheads and channel cats. They tolerate faster water than bullheads but avoid the moderate currents favored by channels. When water levels and velocity are stable, they frequent main channel features like holes and eddies that provide good feeding opportunities and protection from current. During high water, they move away from the main river current to side channels and snag-infested backwaters. They also are found in lakes, ponds, reservoirs and bayous. They are more tolerant of brackish water than the previously mentioned cats.

FOOD HABITS. Although fish such as shad and alewives are their major food, whites also eat aquatic insects, small crustaceans, fish eggs and pondweed. They sometimes feed at night but are not as nocturnal as other catfish.

POPULARITY. Despite their confusion with other cats, white catfish are certainly worthy of your attention. They're fun to catch, especially on light tackle, and eagerly take a wide variety of baits. And if you live in southern New England, they may be the only catfish readily available except bullheads.

They are a favorite of fisheries managers for stocking in fee- or kids'-fishing ponds and lakes, because of their willingness to bite, daytime feeding habits and excellent-tasting flesh.

Bullheads

Bullheads receive a little begrudging admiration now and then, but their name still isn't dropped by anglers looking for status. In fact, they are almost entirely ignored in many areas where they are extremely common.

There are six species of North American bullheads. The black, yellow and brown bullhead are the three of interest to anglers. Within their range they are abundant and grow to a harvestable size. Three other bullheads – the flat, snail and spotted bullhead – rarely exceed a foot in length, and their range is confined to small portions of the southeastern United States. Consequently, these bullheads rate low as gamefish.

COMMON NAMES. Horned pout, greaser, slick, polliwog, polly, paperskin, mudcat, creek cat, stinger, snapper, butterball, bullcat and bullpout.

FOOD HABITS. Bullheads are the fish world's equivalent of barnyard hogs, feeding on a wide range of live and dead offerings just like their larger cousin, the channel cat. Even Henry David Thoreau noticed their indiscriminate feeding behavior. "They will take any kind of bait," he wrote, "from angleworms to a piece of tomato can, without hesitation or coquetry, and they seldom fail to swallow the hook."

Some very impressive creels are taken from the muddiest water. Bullheads tolerate high levels of turbidity better than most gamefish, and since they feed primarily by taste and smell, low visibility isn't a problem. They are also the most tolerant of low oxygen levels.

REPRODUCTION. Eggs are deposited in a nest, usually adjacent to a submerged object. One or both parents take part in building the nest, and take turns caring for the eggs, which may number 2,000 to 4,000 and hatch in 5 to 10 days. The male guards the eggs and fry.

POPULARITY. Many folks love bullheads. They are widely stocked, especially in small urban waters. And in some midwestern states, they are reportedly the number-one ranked fish in terms of numbers taken.

One of the nicest things about bullhead fishing is that it calls for a maximum of sitting and socializing and a minimum of the frenetic foolishness that "fancier" fish demand. Kids of all ages enjoy the thrills, the laughs, the delectable meals and, most of all, the companionship a bullhead junket provides.

Black Bullhead
(Ameiurus melas)

DESCRIPTION. Black bullheads are dark, robust, small-eyed catfish with a square to slightly notched tail, usually with a pale bar at the base. Adults are solid brownish yellow to black, but have no mottling. The anal fin is rounded, and has 17 to 21 rays, with a gray base. Barbels are gray to black

Black Bullhead

in color. The pectoral spines have weakly developed barbs along the rear edge.

RANGE. This species occurs from southern Canada, the Great Lakes and the St. Lawrence River south to the Gulf of Mexico, and from Montana and New Mexico east to the Appalachians. Introduced west of the Rockies.

SIZE. The all-tackle record is 8 pounds, 15 ounces, a giant taken in 1987 from Sturgis Pond in Michigan. Most weigh between 3/4-pound and 2 pounds.

AGE & GROWTH. Black bullheads have a high reproductive rate, which in most bodies of water leads to overcrowding and slow growth. On average, a 4-year-old fish measures 10 inches in length. Few live beyond 5 years of age.

HABITAT. Black bullheads are common residents of ponds, lakes, streams and swamps that have relatively murky water and soft bottoms. They often are the only fish present in freeze-out lakes, since they can tolerate low oxygen levels. They are most active when the water temperature is 75° to 85°F.

Yellow Bullhead
(Ameiurus natalis)

DESCRIPTION. Yellow bullheads closely resemble black bullheads, with a squat body and a slightly rounded to square tail, but differ in having white chin barbels and an anal fin with a straighter edge and 24 to 27 rays. Also, the base of their tail lacks the pale bar. Adults have a solid yellowish to brownish or black body with no mottling. The belly is white.

Yellow Bullhead

RANGE. Yellow bullheads are widespread, occurring throughout the eastern and central United States, and have been introduced in the West and Southwest.

SIZE. A 4.5-pounder caught in Mormon Lake, Arizona, in 1989 is the largest taken on rod and reel. Their average size is similar to black bullheads.

AGE & GROWTH. Unlike black bullheads, yellows rarely reach dense population levels, so they have normal growth rates. A typical 14-inch fish weighs about a pound and a half and is 4 to 5 years old. They live up to 7 years.

HABITAT. Yellow bullheads tend to inhabit smaller, cleaner, weedier bodies of water than their cousins. They are common in areas of dense vegetation in shallow, clear bays of lakes, ponds and slow-moving streams. They prefer water temperatures from 75° to 80°F.

Brown Bullhead
(Ameiurus nebulosus)

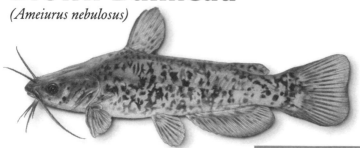

Brown Bullhead

DESCRIPTION. The sides of brown bullheads usually have a distinct, irregular brownish mottling over a light background. The degree of mottling, however, is highly variable. The belly is creamy white. A southern subspecies has more distinct mottling. Brown bullheads differ from the black bullhead in having well-developed barbs on their pectoral spines and 21 to 24 anal fin rays. Unlike the yellow bullhead, their chin barbels are pigmented gray to black.

RANGE. Brown bullheads are found throughout the eastern half of the United States and into southern Canada. Widely introduced into the western states.

SIZE. Average size is larger than the black or yellow bullhead; from 1½ to 3 pounds. The 6-pound, 2-ounce world-record came from Mississippi's Pearl River in 1991.

AGE & GROWTH. Brown bullheads are known to live to 12 years of age. Fish in the North grow much slower than those in the South. A 12-inch fish is 4 to 5 years old and weighs about a pound.

HABITAT. Brown bullheads prefer moderately clear, heavily vegetated streams and lakes and are often found in larger and deeper bodies of water than their cousins. They are also found in ponds and slow-moving streams. Brown bullheads prefer water temperatures between 78° and 82°F, but they can survive in water well over 90°F. They are one of the most-sought members of the bullhead clan.

41

Other Catfish

n addition to the "big three" – channel cat, blue and flathead – 42 species of catfish inhabit waters of the United States and Canada.

The Yaqui catfish *(Ictalurus pricei)* of northwest Mexico and extreme southeast Arizona reaches lengths approaching 2 feet. It is rare, however, and protected in the United States as a threatened species. The headwater catfish *(Ictalurus lupus)* grows to 19 inches but is restricted to the Rio Grande drainage in New Mexico and Texas. Both these fish are almost identical in appearance to the channel catfish.

Twenty-six of our native catfish are madtoms *(genus Noturus)*, most of which are less than 4 inches long. Many are common; some are endangered. They inhabit a variety of waters in the eastern two-thirds of the United States.

Our most unusual cats, perhaps, are the widemouth blindcat *(Satan eurystomus)* and the toothless blindcat *(Trogloglanis pattersoni)*. Both are white and eyeless, inhabiting subterranean waters more than 1/4 mile beneath San Antonio, Texas. They are known from five artesian wells in that area.

The walking catfish *(Clarias batrachus)* is also unusual. It has an air-breathing organ made of modified gill filaments and can walk over land on rainy nights, using the tips of its stout pectoral spines as pivots as it shoves itself along by flexing its body. This Asian native was introduced into Florida waters in the late 1960s. It is abundant in southern and central parts of the state and is thriving despite periodic dieoffs caused by cold weather. Four species of suckermouth catfishes *(Hypostomus* and *Pterygoplichthys)* from Central and South America also are established in United States waters – two in Florida, one in Nevada and one in Texas.

OCEAN CATS. Two species of catfish are caught by anglers fishing saltwater. The gafftopsail catfish *(Bagre marinus)* is found throughout the Gulf of Mexico and in the western Atlantic from the Carolinas to Brazil. The sea, or hardhead catfish *(Arius felis)* is common in Gulf waters and ranges along the Atlantic coast from Cape Cod to the West Indies.

Gafftopsail catfish are so named because of their unusual dorsal and pectoral fins. Each fin is tipped with a long stringlike filament that lends the appearance of a "gafftopsail," a small triangular sail used on some ocean-going vessels. One nickname for the fish is "sailboat."

A gafftop in the 5- to 6-pound range is considered a heavyweight, with most averaging 1 to 2 pounds. The all-tackle world record, an 8-pound, 14-ounce fish, was caught in Florida's Indian River in 1996.

Gafftops often gather in large schools in brackish bays and estuaries where salt concentrations are in the intermediate range, 5 to 30 parts per thousand. But during periods of extended cold, few are reported by inshore fishermen. Gafftops are sensitive to cold and migrate offshore during the worst part of winter. Large die-offs may occur during sudden cold snaps.

The long filamentous extensions on the fins of gafftops distinguish these catfish unmistakably from their relatives the sea cats, which are often caught in the same areas. Sea cats lack this unusual ornamentation. The chin barbels also help anglers separate the two species: gafftops have two; sea cats, four.

The sea cat is one of the smallest rod-and-reel catfish in North American waters. Sixteen or 17 inches is close to the maximum length. One-half to 1 pound is the average size in most areas, with rare individuals topping 2 pounds. The waters off Sebastian, Florida, produced the biggest thus far recorded in world-record listings, a 3-pound, 5-ounce sea cat caught in 1993.

Sea cats are more likely to be taken in areas where salinity is high, 30 or more parts per thousand. Schools often gather around oil platforms, barrier islands, artificial reefs and other offshore structure. During warm weather, young sea cats may migrate to brackish waters and often travel upstream in coastal creeks, rivers and canals.

The spawning habits of gafftops and sea cats are amazing. Following courtship, the male takes the large (3/4- to 1-inch diameter) eggs into his mouth for incubation. The eggs hatch in 60 to 70 days, during which time the male does not eat. The male continues protecting the fry by carrying them in his mouth until they are about 3 inches long. Up to 55 eggs or 27 young may be held in the male's mouth.

Ocean cats can be caught around the clock, but like fresh-water catfish, they're primarily nocturnal feeders. The best fishing is at night. They hit hard and fight a strong, dogged battle, especially when taken on light tackle. Both species often move in large schools, so if a fisherman hooks one, there's an excellent chance more are nearby.

IN THE WATERS of mid-America swims another large, smooth-skinned fish often called catfish. It's proper name is paddlefish (Polyodon spathula), but many anglers know it as the spoonbill catfish, shovelnose cat or boneless cat. Despite popular misconceptions, it is not a catfish at all. In fact, this prehistoric creature is more closely related to sharks than catfish. It is found mostly in large rivers, such as the Mississippi, Missouri and Ohio, and their tributaries.

Spoonbill Catfish?

The paddlefish is the fish world's equivalent of Pinocchio. The most noticeable feature of this unusual fish is its weird nose. Protruding like a built-in boat paddle between its beady eyes is a misshapen snoot as a long as a child's arm.

Other curious features enhance the comic-book image. The paddlefish has no bones, only cartilage. The skin is leathery and scaleless. The tail is sickle-shaped like a shark's. And while the paddlefish may weigh over 150 pounds, it feeds only on microscopic animals (zooplankton) siphoned through a toothless mouth big enough to engulf a basketball.

In states where they are still common, paddlefish are popular quarry for anglers. Snagging is the only reliable method for catching them since they don't take bait. Many are caught by anglers snagging for catfish.

WHERE TO FIND
CATFISH

Typical Catfish Waters

Catfish evolved in the currents of our rivers and streams, and, in these waters, they usually reach their greatest numbers and largest size. Catfish adapt better than most freshwater species, however, and their natural ranges have been greatly expanded by stocking programs. Today they exist in waters of all shapes and sizes, from tiny farm ponds and creeks to the Great Lakes and the Mississippi River. Every state except Alaska is home to at least one of the "big three" species – channel, flathead and blue.

The types of waters where catfish are not found are relatively few. They rarely thrive in cold, fast-running streams

where trout are abundant. Nor do they do well in the cold, oligotrophic lakes of the Far North. Mesotrophic lakes with large walleye populations may support good channel cat and/or bullhead populations, but blues and flatheads usually are absent or scarce, and channel cat numbers never reach their full potential. With the exception of white cats, all our freshwater catfish are intolerant of brackish and salt water.

Almost everywhere else, thriving populations of catfish are found. Big fertile rivers. Bayous. Large, man-made impoundments. Oxbow lakes. Creeks. City water-supply lakes. Sloughs. Irrigation canals. Ponds. Smallmouth streams. State wildlife agency lakes. River backwaters. Strip pits. Overflows. Clear water, muddy water, warm water, cool water and everything in between – if it's not too polluted, catfish of one form or another are likely to call it home.

Typical catfish waters? As you can see, there's no such thing. Our adaptable catfish have a remarkable ability to thrive wherever they may be.

Small to Mid-Size Rivers

In small to mid-size rivers, catfish tend to be small to mid-size, too. There are exceptions, of course, but if you're after a trophy, this is not the type of water to focus on. Although channel cats are the primary species found in these rivers, flatheads and blues can also be present, especially in the lower ends.

North America is covered by countless miles of rivers, most of which fall into this category. Not all of these contain catfish, however. Certain characteristics of a river determine whether it is suitable for cats. Among the most important of these are gradient and bottom composition.

Gradient is the slope of the streambed, which determines current speed and bottom composition. Rivers with a high gradient have a fast current and a hard, rocky bottom; those with a low gradient are slow-moving and have a soft, silty bottom. Channel catfish are most abundant in rivers that fall in between these two extremes, those with a moderate flow, meandering stream course and rock-gravel bottom. Flatheads tend to do best in slower-moving streams with abundant woody cover. Although blues inhabit these stream types, they seldom are found in any numbers.

In areas where rock and gravel underlie a stream, these rivers form a series of rapids and pools. Understanding these structures and how catfish relate to them can improve your fishing.

RAPIDS-POOL. Rapids (1) form over hard bottom and are shallower than other spots in the river because water can't erode the bottom material. The gradient is higher here, and often the river is narrower, causing the water to move faster. You can see the rapids because the water boils up, and it is often so shallow there are exposed rocks.

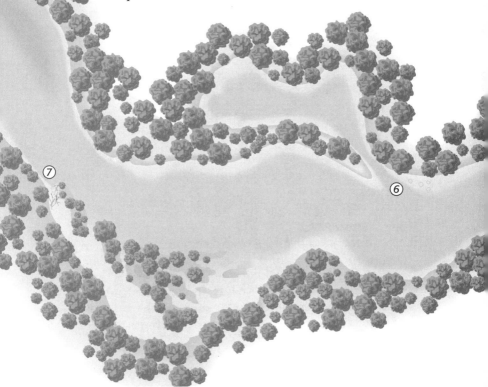

Below the rapids, the fast water carves the channel deeper. The water through this stretch is quite turbulent, often creating standing waves and whitecaps. This is where the *pool* forms, an area of slower-moving water that may be several yards to a half mile long. At the head of most pools, there is a depression, or hole (2). The rapids' churning water scours the bottom here, creating the deepest part of the pool.

Below each hole, the river's flow slows. Sediments fall, and the downstream end of the pool gets shallower, until the water encounters another area of hard bottom. Another rapids forms, and the sequence begins again. Rapids, pool. Rapids, pool.

Holes within a pool are the best places to catch catfish. Cats travel through rapids when moving from one part of a river to another and sometimes make short forays to these areas to feed. They seldom stay very long, however. Holes, on the other hand, provide depth, current, food and security – everything catfish need to feel at home. The hole's deepest portion is the den, or bedroom area, where cats can rest out of the current. The upper end is the kitchen, where cats feed.

Rocks, logs and fallen trees in the deeper, upstream end of the hole make it even more attractive to catfish. Cats wait in ambush behind these current breaks, darting out to gobble up food, or bait, that passes by. Cover objects in portions of the hole where current is less or water is shallow aren't as likely to hold catfish.

When rivers of this size run through bottomlands where rock and gravel are limited, the rapids-pool structure is much harder to discern. It is present to some extent, and cats still favor the deepest holes. In this situation, a depth finder can be extremely beneficial for determining the best fishing spots.

CURRENT SEAMS. These are created where fast and slow water merge (3). Baitfish and other food items collect along the seams. Catfish gather in the slower portion of the seam to take advantage of these conditions. Current seams form downstream of bridge piers, big snags, logjams, shoreline points, large boulders and islands. Tributary junctions usually have two seams, one on the upstream edge and one on the downstream edge. Work baits along the slower edge of the seam for the best action.

EDDIES. These form where current reverses direction due to water deflecting off a shoreline point or other obstruction (4). At the point where the current reverses, a mini-vortex – the eddy – develops. Like current seams, the slower water around the eddy provides an ideal ambush point for hungry catfish.

BOULDERS. Large boulders may be difficult to find in deep water without electronics, but shallow ones should be visible to the naked eye. Most active cats are near bottom on the upstream edge of boulders, with a few positioning near the crown and boil-line areas. Cats in slack water behind boulders are usually inactive.

LOW-HEAD DAMS. These (5) were built on many small rivers back in the 1940s and 1950s as flood control structures. They are a barrier to fish migration, so in late winter and into spring catfish can be found in their greatest numbers below a low-head dam. A large scour hole forms just below the apron of the dam where the current flows over. This slack-water area is where the majority of the catfish hold.

The best way to fish a low-head dam is to anchor well downstream of it and make a long cast up to the slack-water area below the turbulent water. Avoid a positioning too close to the dam; the powerful undertow can suck even a large boat under.

CHANNELS TO BACKWATERS. On streams with adjacent backwater areas, the channel (6) connecting the two can be a great catfish magnet, especially when the channel has some current. Focus your efforts on backwater channels that are at least 4 feet deep, have cover such as stumps or rocks, and lead to a backwater that has deep enough water to draw feeding or spawning catfish.

A good time to fish these channels is just after the spawn when hungry fish are moving out of the backwaters, or during a slow rise or fall of the main river. Backwaters and channels that remain deep nearly year-round are good ones to fish at night, because big fish that are on the move feeding frequent these areas.

LOGJAMS. In slow, meandering streams, logjams or *snags* (7), as they're often called, are the primary habitat for catfish. This kind of cover can be as simple as a downed tree or log in the river, or as complex as multiple dead trees that have washed downstream and hung in an outside bend.

As a rule, the best snags are large, consist of multiple trees and branches, and are found in water deeper than 3 feet. A logjam of this size can hold numbers of catfish, especially if it is located in deep water. Smaller snags such as a single tree or branch may hold only one or two fish.

In rivers where logjams are the primary habitat, catfish can be found in them nearly year-round.

To catch catfish in small to mid-size rivers, it's also important to understand seasonal movements that occur. During some seasons, catfish may be almost totally absent from long stretches of water. It helps to understand why, and where they go.

A study conducted in the lower Platte River in Nebraska, a tributary of the Missouri River, exemplifies the movement patterns existing in many such waters. Thirty-eight adult channel cats implanted with radio transmitters were released and tracked. Their movements showed distinct seasonal trends.

According to the researchers, their movement patterns suggest downstream movement in the fall and winter to deep scour pools in the Missouri River, where the fish overwinter. In spring, there was a heavy movement upstream to spawning and feeding areas, where they spend the summer. These movements are most likely in response to changing temperature and/or discharge patterns in the river.

The researchers also discovered that juvenile catfish prefer areas of intermediate depth, while adults favor the deepest water available. Both life stages tend to use areas having slow to moderate current velocities. Adult channel catfish have a strong preference for areas with log snags and rock revetments along the banks of the river. These structures create areas of deep, slow-velocity water where adult catfish can find a refuge underneath or behind an object.

Studies in other areas suggest blue and flathead catfish also undergo seasonal migrations of this sort. And while we can't say channel catfish always behave the same in other waters, the movements described above are similar to those observed in many other small to mid-size rivers.

Applying knowledge of these movements can help anglers determine where catfish are most likely to be throughout the seasons, thus increasing the chance of catching fish.

PRIME CATFISH HABITAT IN SMALL TO MID-SIZE RIVERS

•*Side channels* connect backwater lakes and sloughs to the main channel. Deep ones are usually more productive than shallow ones. The best time to fish these is when a light current is moving out of the backwater into the river.

•*Current seams* form where fast and slow water meet, usually below a rapids, a shoreline point or an outside bend of a river. Catfish hold in the slow water and dart into the fast water to feed on baitfish and other food items.

•*Low-head dams* block upstream fish movements, so fish tend to concentrate in the deep hole that forms just below, especially in the spring. Catfish can be caught below them year-round.

•*Holes* are one of the best locations to catch catfish in these types of rivers. The most productive ones are found on an outside bend of the river and have structure present on the upstream side, such as timber or large boulders. Holes are also found midstream just below a stretch of rapids, or just downstream of man-made structures such as dams and bridges.

•*Logjams* hold catfish nearly year-round. The best ones are in water deeper than 3 feet, are large and are made up of multiple trees or logs. As a rule, the bigger the logjam, the more fish it can hold.

Big Rivers

Catfish and big rivers go hand in hand. Some of the best catfishing today is on big rivers. They offer diverse habitat, plenty of food and ideal spawning habitat for catfish, and miles of fishable water and trophy potential for catfishermen.

For the first-time big-river fisherman, deciding where to fish can be somewhat intimidating. But once you know what to look for, most big-river hot spots are easy to find; just use your eyes. Finding some areas requires use of a boat, map and/or electronic equipment, but most catfish habitat is readily visible and much of it is accessible from shore.

Big-river cats position themselves at strategic places to feed and rest, usually near structure that breaks or reduces current. Resting fish prefer areas with little

56

current. Moderate current is preferred when feeding by ambush. Actively feeding cats often use areas of heavy current, but current-breaking structure is usually nearby.

Understanding these facts is the catter's key to reading big rivers. Following are the best areas to find cats in big rivers.

WING DAMS. These are also called wing dikes, and are among the best big-river spots. Wing dams (1) are long, narrow rock structures on rivers with barge traffic. They are built perpendicular to the bank and direct current into the

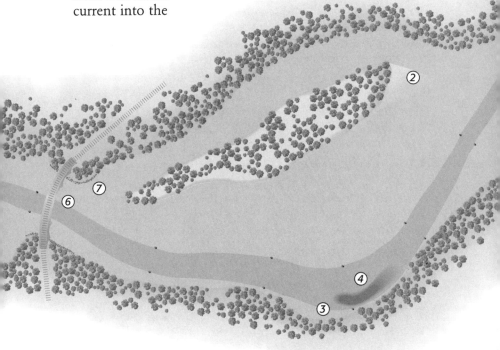

main channel to keep it from silting in. They also reduce shoreline erosion. They're most numerous immediately below dams but may be scattered along the entire length of a big river.

Most active catfish hold near the bottom on the wing dam's upstream side. Reduced current exists in this area along the length of the dam. Some fish are found along the top of the dam, and in the boil-line over and just downstream from the wing dam's crown. Less active cats move to deeper scour holes, usually near the channel end of the dam. These fish are usually tough to catch.

When fishing wing dams, look for subtle changes in structure on or near the dam. A fallen tree, large boulder or other object often attracts cats.

BARS. Rock, gravel and sandbars (2) – common in most large rivers – are good catfishing areas when water is high and current strong. For this reason, it pays to learn the location of bars when water is low and they are exposed.

Catfish gather around bars to avoid excessive current and are common when concentrations of food are available. In the lower Mississippi River, for instance, thousands of small leeches "hatch" from sandbars in late summer, attracting enormous schools of channel catfish. Rock and gravel bars on the lower Arkansas River harbor dense populations of crayfish when spring's high water begins to recede. Catfish gather to feed on these seasonal banquets.

When the water level falls, the tops of bars may be exposed. When this happens, catfish and forage animals move to deeper sections of the bar, usually near the channel end.

OUTSIDE RIVER BENDS. These are exceptional cat attractors. Along outside bends (3), the river is usually deeper, and the current gouges into the bank, forming undercuts. These areas offer seclusion to hole-loving flatheads and other catfish waiting to ambush prey.

Outside bends attract catfish for other reasons, too. As the river eats away at the bank, trees topple into the water. This timber provides excellent current-breaking cover for catfish and the baitfish they feed on. If a deep hole lies just downstream from the fallen timber, the area is even better. The existence of current, cover and food with deep water nearby makes this one of the best spots to find big-river cats.

HOLES. Although difficult to pinpoint at times, potholes or depressions in the bottom of a river are first-rate places to try for catfish.

Holes usually occur directly below rapids where current washes away the bottom, or on the outside bend of the river (4). Like mid-size rivers, big rivers can have a rapids-pool configuration, but not as pronounced. Sometimes, a hole is found midstream, with no apparent reason for its presence. A sonar unit and/or contour map aids in locating holes.

If a hole is deep, fish near the upstream edge of its rim. Active catfish are likely to be feeding here. Cats in deeper portions of a hole are often inactive.

If the structure is shallow – more of a depression than a hole – catfish may be found anywhere in it, but usually they're near the upstream edge. Work the depression thoroughly until you locate fish.

HUMPS. These structures always merit the catter's attention. Unless they rise close to the surface, they are difficult to find without electronics. Those with shallow tops can be located by looking for the boil-line that forms above them.

At night and on cloudy or rainy days, catfish move on top of humps to feed on baitfish attracted to the structure. This is a great place to fish on hot summer nights. During the day, look for cats positioned on sides of the hump that are shaded, or near deep edges where light penetration and current are reduced.

TRIBUTARIES. Tributary creeks and streams (5) provide staging areas for catfish during pre-spawn and post-spawn periods. If the mouth of the feeder stream is relatively deep at its confluence with the main river, or if the tributary channel joins the main river channel, the area can be good year-round. A great deal depends on water depth, water temperature, available structure and food availability.

During cool months, catfish may move into tributaries if the incoming water is warmer. Tributary mouths are also good when heavy rains flush food into the river. Gravel bars that form at the mouths of many tributaries also provide good catfish habitat. Difference in water clarity may also attract cats to tributaries. For example, flatheads may make short forays from a big, muddy, rain-swollen river into the clearer, more stable water of a small tributary. This behavior is sparked by movements of their favorite foods, which enter the smaller creek to escape the heavy current. Catfish themselves often are attracted to less turbid waters of a small, deep, clear-running tributary.

CHUTES. Deep-water chutes are overlooked by many catters, but often hold heavy concentrations of trophy-class catfish. Chutes occur where a river narrows, such as splitting to go around an island or other midstream obstruction. Cats gather near the upstream and downstream edges of the chute where current slackens, especially where gravel bars or other current breaks are present.

Move to one end of the chute or the other, and pay out line a few feet at a time, allowing the bait to drift near bottom. Stop the bait occasionally and allow it to remain stationary a few minutes. If no pickups occur, release more line and repeat the process.

MAIN CHANNEL. Many rivers have a distinct channel that may intersect many of the features already mentioned. Any structure near the main channel that breaks current is likely to hold cats.

The edge of the channel also is a key area. A shallow lip usually connects the deepest portion of the channel to a shallow river flat. Cats often roam these flats at night searching for food. When not on the flats, they tend to hold along the edge where the flat and the channel meet. These are key areas for anglers to contact channel cats and smaller blues. Big blues often hold at the base of the channel drop. Big flatheads also move into these deep areas but prefer less current than blues.

BRIDGES. In summer, catfish frequently hold around bridge pilings (6). These offer shaded water with less current where aquatic invertebrates and baitfish are found in abundance. With sonar, you can ease along the pilings and determine the depth and position of any fish schools. Once located, back your boat away from the bridge, and cast a slightly weighted bait past a piling, letting it slowly drift down to the fish.

RIPRAP. After fishing bridge pilings, work riprap lining the adjacent shore (7). These are man-made stretches of rock that prevent bank erosion. Cast parallel to the bank, starting fairly deep and gradually working deeper as you move away from the bank. Live crayfish are hard baits to beat around riprap.

DAM TAILRACES. Catfish of all species congregate year-round in the churning tailwaters of big-river dams (8). Few places offer a better chance for taking trophy cats.

Tailrace catfishing is good for several reasons. All catfish are somewhat migratory and undertake seasonal movements. Astounding concentrations gather in tailwaters because their movements are impeded by dams.

Abundant baitfish are another attraction. Shad, skipjack herring and other forage fish like the well-oxygenated water and are also stopped in their upstream movement. Tailraces concentrate baitfish, thus providing catfish plenty to eat. Also, baitfish sucked through turbines come into the tailwaters injured or cut up and provide an easy meal. Regular water flow keeps oxygen levels high, an important consideration during hot weather when slow-moving water downstream may be low in oxygen content.

Big catfish, especially big blues, are drawn to the swift, churning water below a dam. To conserve energy, however, they seek slack-water holding spots, called *grooves*. These are the slower-moving water areas between open gates or running turbines.

When gates or turbines are open, the fastest water is in the center of the discharge; the slowest water is on outer edges of the flow. The surface water all appears to be moving at the same speed, but actually, the area of water between two discharges – the groove – is slower-moving. Fishing these grooves is far more productive than fishing heavier current.

If cats quit biting in one groove, move to another. Water flow through a dam fluctuates as power requirements or water levels demand. So even though water runs continuously, the volume of flow may change several times daily. When the flow changes, cats often move, seeking slacker water.

LOCKS. In many big rivers, a locking system (9) is constructed adjacent the dam so boats can move upstream and downstream. Each time a boat is locked through, water is pumped in or out of the lock, creating heavy currents that stir up baitfish and other forage. Small catfish, usually channels, often gather in sizable feeding schools in these areas.

Since locks are near one bank or another, you can fish from shore. Cast your bait against the lock wall, letting it roll into the water below. The best fishing is usually when the lock is being filled or emptied, but catfish may remain in shady lock-wall areas throughout the day and night. Fishing can be good even during midday hours.

OTHER FACTORS. Reading big rivers involves more than finding fish structure. Good river anglers also pay attention to changing water levels and seasonal patterns. Here are some factors to consider.

A muddy, fast-rising river intimidates many anglers, but under these circumstances, the cat bite may be extraordinary due to the abundance of forage stirred about in the roiling current. When the river begins to fall, the bite may cease until conditions stabilize.

When fishing below a dam, avoid periods when gates are closed and current is nil. Under such conditions, baitfish are absent, and catfishing is rarely productive.

Big-river cats are somewhat transient, moving from one area to another as seasons change. In summer and winter, extremes of heat and cold drive them to deep areas, such as holes or the main river channel. Spring and autumn offer more moderate water temperatures, allowing catfish to invade shallow, off-channel areas. During these seasons, they're often in backwaters, river-connected oxbows and other areas with little current. Tailwaters and tributaries draw heavy cat concentrations during spring spawning runs and when water conditions are poor in other reaches.

PRIME CATFISH HABITAT IN BIG RIVERS

•*Wing dams* are present on rivers that have barge traffic. Catfish hold on the upstream and downstream side as well as the scour hole that forms off the end.

•*Tailraces* congregate catfish that are moving upstream. They are best in the spring when most fish are on the move, but can be good year-round.

•*Bridge pilings* create a current break, forming a slack-water pocket on their downstream side. Those found in deep water often harbor trophy catfish.

•*Tributaries* bring food items into the main river after heavy rains, which attract catfish to the mouth. Larger tributaries are also used for spawning.

•*Grooves* are slack-water areas found between two open gates of a dam. Catfish hold in the slow water and dart out into the current to feed.

•*Riprap banks,* especially long, irregular ones, are great catfish hideouts. Cats use cavities between rocks to spawn, but good stretches are used year-round.

Man-Made Lakes

Reservoirs are found throughout North America, and take on many different forms – everything from warm, shallow and fertile to cold, clear and deep. Catfish inhabit many types of reservoirs, but reach their greatest numbers and size in bodies of water that are large, warm and fertile with plentiful cover near deepwater sanctuaries and shallow feeding areas. In fact, some of the biggest catfish caught in recent history have come from man-made lakes. For consistent action on reservoirs, you need to key on specific areas. Here are the most important.

⑤

OLD RIVER CHANNELS.
   Some man-made lakes have easily definable river channels (1), while others have only subtle drops. Both are catfish magnets. A good depth finder is invaluable in locating these channels. In many reservoirs, the main channel acts like a major highway, leading migrating catfish from one part of the impoundment to another. Intersecting creek channels act as "secondary roads" leading fish up these creek arms toward shoreline areas.

Catfish hold in deep water that falls off into the channel. The best drops, or *ledges*, have structure nearby – a brush pile, a point, an adjacent hump or a pocket cutting into the bank. While some cats relate to the top of a ledge, the biggest prefer the deep water at the base. They're also

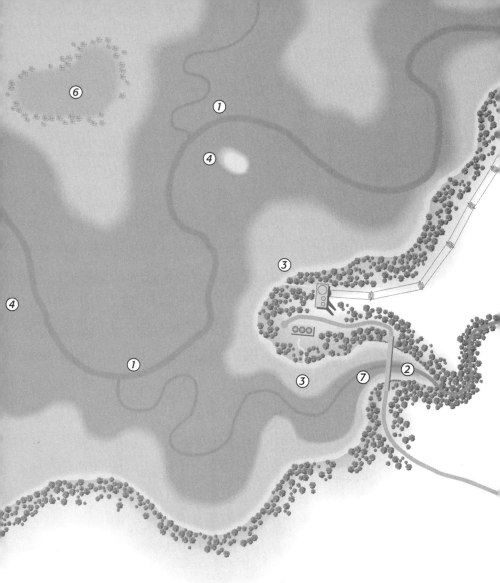

found at channel junctions, the outside turns of channels and deep channel edges near the dam.

TRIBUTARIES. The mouth of a creek or river (2) can be a real glory hole when conditions are right, such as during the pre-spawn period and after heavy rains. In early spring, an incoming creek usually brings warmer water that attracts baitfish and, consequently, catfish. During summer, the mouths of coolwater streams draw catfish, especially at night. Fish behind a current break – a hump, hole or tree – near the stream mouth.

POWER PLANTS. Electric generating facilities are common on many impoundments. Catfish hold near the mouths of discharge (3) and inlet channels, as well as out into the lake where there's still a hint of moving water. In some reservoirs the current hugs the shore; in others it curves out into the main lake. Once you figure out the current pattern, fish the seams where the moving and slack water meet. Warm-water discharges attract huge numbers of shad and other baitfish in late fall and winter, when the water temperature in the lake drops. Catfish follow, feeding on dead and dying baitfish.

HUMPS. These can be the most productive catfishing spots in reservoirs, especially during the hot summer months. A contour map combined with a depth finder is key to find-ing humps. The best ones are 5 to 20 feet down, have tim-ber, rocks or brush on them and have deep water nearby (4).

Once a hump is pinpointed, learn all you can about it – its size, the steepness of drops, and existing cover. Narrow your fishing area to a few choice zones – points, pockets, rock beds, timbered areas, etc. – then mark them with buoys.

RIPRAP. Many impoundments have long stretches of riprap along their shorelines (5). Catfish are drawn to these rocky areas because they hold crayfish, shad and other forage. Riprap also provides cavities for spawning. Look for riprap near dams or by bridges, causeways and roads crossing nar-row channels.

When fishing a long stretch of riprap, key on specific objects, such as an old tree, a culvert or even a change in the size of rocks. Look for unusual bottom features at the base of the riprap with a depth finder. Creek channels or old roadbeds close to shore, or sunken brush are prime catfish hideouts.

INUNDATED LAKES AND PONDS. Small ponds and lakes often are flooded when a large reservoir is created (6). These can be especially productive in shallow reservoirs. A topo map used in conjunction with a depth finder is essential to find these. Once located, look for points and dropoffs just as you would on any lake. Sunken islands in the old lake bed are also key spots. If scattered trees or stumps exist around the edge of the submerged pond, fish them carefully.

BRIDGES. These attract catfish during hot weather. The deep, shaded channel below (7) provides cool water, and the pilings are covered with algae that attract aquatic invertebrates and small fish. Most cats hold near the pilings and often suspend at mid-depths.

Knowing seasonal movements is important when fishing reservoir catfish. Like their river relatives, these fish move from season to season, but not as drastically. For example, deep wintering areas and spawning grounds may only be 100 yards apart in a man-made lake, as opposed to 10 miles in a river.

The biggest movement is in spring when catfish leave deep winter haunts and filter into the shallows to spawn. This is triggered by longer days and water temperatures warming above 70°F. This may be as early as April in the South and as late as July in the North.

Pre-spawn rates among the best of the year for fast-paced cat catching. Catfish are ravenous after weeks on limited rations and easy to catch with well-placed baits. Many reservoir cats follow channels toward shoreline shallows where spawning sites like muskrat holes, undercut banks and hollows are found. Others run up tributary streams searching for similar sites.

During the spawn, catfishing takes a nosedive for a few weeks. Fortunately, not all catfish spawn at the same time. At any one time, some are busy spawning, some are recuperating and others are feeding. The feeders can be caught.

After spawning, catfish start to move and feed again. Those in tributaries either move downstream and back into the lake or linger near the spawning area if good habitat is present. Cats that spawn in the reservoir usually return to deeper water, near cover with fast-breaking bottom structure such as humps and channel edges. Most rest in deep areas during the day and feed in shallows at night.

If the reservoir stratifies in summer, catfish move to shallower structures in or near the thermocline where oxygen levels and water temperature are favorable. But when the thermocline disappears during fall turnover, most cats move back to deep water.

Oxbow Lakes

In many physical respects, oxbows are vastly different from man-made lakes, and each oxbow has characteristics that make it different from others. Unless one knows and understands these differences, catfishing may be nothing more than an exercise in futility. To better understand the variables that influence oxbow catfishing, let's examine the origins and physical attributes of oxbow lakes.

OXBOW ORIGINS. Over the years, lowland rivers constantly change course, always following the path of least resistance. As a river meanders, it erodes the shores of its outside bends, and loops of water are severed from the main stream. The ends of the loops eventually are blocked by sediments deposited by the parent stream, and a crescent-shaped lake is left behind. The shape of these lakes resembles the U-shaped piece of wood on an ox yoke, and thus they are called oxbow lakes. They also are known as "cutoffs" or "river lakes."

When an oxbow is cut off from the river, its character immediately begins changing. Sediment carried in from seasonal flooding builds up, and the old meander scar becomes shallower and relatively flat-bottomed. Water-tolerant plants like cypress, tupelo, buckbrush and willow take root along the lake's edges. In years of drought, some shallow oxbows dry up, allowing plants to gain a foothold and encroach still farther into the lake.

All these natural processes, from the cutting off of a new oxbow to the building of bottom sediment to the gradual extension of woody vegetation farther and farther from the bank, are stages in the death of an oxbow lake. The process may take 500 years or more, but left undisturbed, all oxbows eventually silt in and turn into a wetland forest.

During this long process of dying, oxbows provide fantastic catfishing. The annual cycle of spring flooding that gradually chokes these lakes with silt also makes them the outstanding fisheries they are. The flooding cycle stimulates oxbow cats to go on a feeding binge as waters recede to normal levels. The feeding binge puts them in excellent spawning condition, and because of the fertility of river oxbows, heavy spawns usually follow each winter/spring flooding cycle. Spawning still occurs in years of

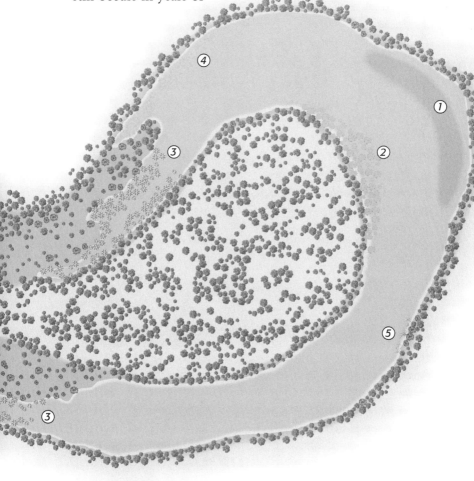

drought, when flooding is absent, but it doesn't happen with the gusto that characterizes post-flood spawns.

OXBOW TYPES. Mastering oxbow fishing requires knowledge of the types of oxbow lakes. Some oxbows remain seasonally connected to the parent stream; some are not. Those significantly separated from the parent stream are only affected during major floods.

Oxbows connected to the main river normally provide the best catfishing. When the river floods the oxbow, inflowing nutrients enrich the water and help sustain thriving communities of forage animals on which catfish feed. This yearly overflow cycle also provides temporary, but important, spawning habitat for oxbow cats and often replenishes the lake with fish and baitfish from the river.

There are no hard-and-fast rules for fishing river-connected oxbows; fish are caught under all conditions. But as a general rule, catfish seldom bite when the water is on a fast rise. Fishing runout areas – the cuts connecting oxbow and river – can sometimes be outstanding during a fast fall. But the best fishing on connected oxbows is usually when the water level is steady to slowly rising or falling.

On river-connected oxbows, catfishermen should know the depth at which the river overflows the lake being fished. This information is usually available at local bait shops or from area anglers. Monitor the river level in local newspapers to plan a trip during peak fishing periods. When the river is entirely out of the oxbow, water and fishing conditions are likely to be more predictable. When the river overflows into the oxbow, anglers must know the rate of water level fluctuations – fast rise, slow fall, etc. – to determine the best fishing days.

Some oxbows are completely isolated by levees or dams. These lakes usually provide the most predictable fishing opportunities, since water fluctuations are less dramatic. These may be the best oxbows to fish when water conditions are unfavorable elsewhere.

OXBOW HABITAT. Even though most oxbows are relatively flat and of uniform depth, the outside bend (1) of the lake is usually deeper than the inside bend. During summer and winter, cats tend to concentrate on the deeper side of the lake where the temperature and water conditions are more favorable. In most oxbows, the amount of deep water is limited, so you don't have to look far to find fish.

When cats are in the shallows, they relate to some sort of cover. Cypress trees (2) skirt the banks of many southern oxbows, and working natural baits or stinkbaits around their broad bases and knees is a good way to catch cats. Buckbrush and willows (3) also are prevalent on many oxbows, and many cats are caught in the thickest such cover available. Other prime fishing spots include fallen trees, beaver lodges, sunken Christmas tree shelters, lily pads, weedbeds (4), shoreline riprap, stump fields, fallen timber (5), boat docks and duck hunting blinds.

If you're on an oxbow when flood waters are receding, fish around run-out chutes (6) that connect the oxbow and river. These spots are cat magnets. Look for areas where outflowing water is constricted, like sloughs and natural cuts, then work cutbait or live baitfish around surrounding cover. Key your efforts to periods when water is falling 3 to 6 inches a day; a faster fall makes it hard to locate fish.

One final note: when considering where to go, think small. Although some oxbows cover several thousand acres, the real jewels are much smaller. Catfish are harder to pinpoint on large oxbows because there is too much water to cover. For the true oxbow experience, visit small lakes off the beaten path. It's not uncommon to fish all day on one of these little lakes and never see another boat.

Ponds

In most areas, ponds offer excellent fishing for catfish. Channel cats and bullheads adapt especially well to man-made ponds, and are regularly stocked in many states for recreational opportunities. In some areas, ponds may also have blue and flathead catfish.

Ponds offer several advantages over bigger waters. Smaller acreage allows anglers to fish the entire body of water thoroughly and effectively. There are literally millions of ponds throughout the country, so almost every catfish fan can enjoy pond fishing close to home. Unlike bigger, more popular waters, ponds usually aren't crowded and can be fished without a boat, expensive paraphernalia and excessive worrying about wind, current or other complications.

Though pond fishing exemplifies catfish angling at its simplest, there's more to catching pond fish than just wetting a hook. Identifying the correct techniques, presentation, baits and locational factors is important even on these small waters.

By definition, a pond is a body of water smaller than a lake. Size may range anywhere from 1/2 acre to perhaps 20 acres. Like other waters, ponds have such things as structure, vegetation and water clarity that provide keys to catching fish. A pond may be natural or man-made. It may get its water from runoff, an underground spring or a feeder creek. Some have creek channels, some are bowl-shaped. Some are clear, others are muddy. In a nutshell, ponds are quite similar to lakes, but smaller.

Because ponds are small, anglers have fewer problems pinpointing catfish when they are actively feeding. Most ponds are also shallow, so you can probe virtually every level.

Pond catfish often are found near shoreline cover and structure throughout the warm months and into autumn. During periods of temperature extremes, though, especially during midsummer and winter, they frequent the deepest water available, providing there is adequate oxygen. Often, they lie right on the bottom, and given a choice, are near some type of cover. A deep-water area containing an isolated snag is preferred over deep water with no such object.

Fishing directly on the bottom using either natural or stinkbait is a good tactic for catching fish during hot and cold weather. If fishing is slow, "fan-cast" a section of the pond to locate catfish. Make your first cast to your left, placing your bait near the shore. With each successive cast, move in a clockwise direction, placing each cast about 5 feet from the previous cast and continuing in a broad arc. Use whatever number of casts it takes to catch a catfish or to reach the shoreline to your right. If you complete the entire series of casts from bank to bank and still haven't found catfish, move down the shore and start again, covering a new plot of water.

This method helps you cover the pond thoroughly, but you must also remember to cover all depths. Pond catfish feed on the bottom, on top and in between. Catfish raised on a diet of floating fish chow, for example, are especially prone to topside feeding. In some ponds, catfish tend to suspend. If you confine yourself to bottom presentations in such situations, your catch rate may be low.

Start fishing in the deepest water available. On dammed ponds, this is usually near the dam (1). On four-leveed ponds, it may be in the borrow ditch on the pond's perimeter or in another deep hole dug during the pond's construction. In any case, start where water is deepest and try to determine at what depth catfish are located. This is done through a series of fan casts fished at different depths.

On the first series of casts, the bait is allowed to rest directly on the bottom of the pond. If that doesn't produce, add a slip-bobber to your rig and present the bait at mid-depths. During the third series of casts (if necessary), present the bait just a foot or two below the surface, changing the position of the bobber stop to achieve the desired depth.

Creek coves, where feeder creeks enter a pond (2), are good places during spring and early autumn when catfish are ready to invade the shallows. In-flowing creek water also provides relief from extreme summer and winter temperatures. Water coming into the pond is usually a different temperature.

Look for catfish hanging right on the edge of the creek channel. The channel usually runs through the cove and passes somewhere through the mouth of the cove. For thorough coverage, fish both sides of the cove mouth carefully, trying to locate catfish holding along the dropoff the channel creates. Then move back into the cove and fish the spot where the creek enters the pond by fanning a series of casts to cover the entire area.

Vegetation also should get your attention in ponds. Plant cover not only provides food and cover for catfish, it also indicates the bottom structure of the pond. For instance, weed growth commencing along the shoreline (3) and extending out 30 or 40 feet indicates a shallow flat. The bottom may drop sharply where the weedline ends, something worth checking.

Look for small islands of weeds separate from the contour of the shoreline (4), as these are exceptional catfish attractors. Usually one side has deeper water than the other. This is the place to fish, but be sure to place your bait as close to the weedline as possible.

Look, too, for openings in the weedbeds where you can drop in a bait (5). Catfish love these cool, food-rich confines, and any natural bait presented here is likely to be devoured. Any changes in contour (pockets or indentations) along the edge of the weeds should also be investigated.

In sizing up a pond, also look for rock piles, stick-ups, stumps, logs, trees, holes, humps and points. These are typical catfish hot spots and should be fished thoroughly. Any brush or submerged objects offshore (6) deserve special attention, as do docks and piers, deep holes around inflowing water pumps, overhanging and fallen trees (7) and riprap along shore.

3

EQUIPMENT
FOR CATCHING CATFISH

Rods, Reels & Line

Choosing rods, reels and line for catfishing is like buying a vehicle. Numerous styles of each are available, everything from simple and inexpensive to fancy, high-dollar designs with all the bells and whistles. Not everyone wants the same thing.

Catfishermen use a wider variety of rods and reels than any group of sport fishermen – everything from tiny spinning outfits that fit under a car seat to long surf-casting rods with huge reels.

If you spend most of your time dabbling for bullheads in farm ponds, a light spinning or spincasting outfit with small diameter line works great. If channel cats are your quarry, and you fish waters where 5- to 10-pounders sometimes surface, a 6- to 7-foot, medium-action bass-fishing combo is more than adequate. If snagging is your thing, and you're hoping to bring in one of the 100-pounders lurking in a dam tailrace, better go equipped with a 10- to 16-foot heavy-duty saltwater baitcasting rig spooled with 40- or 50-pound line.

It all boils down to using common sense when shopping. Look at the options available, then buy the best combination you can afford for the conditions and catfish you encounter.

Rods

Almost any rod can be used to fish catfish, but some styles have qualities that make them better for catfishing than others. Things to consider when buying a cat rod include length, composition and quality.

LENGTH. Long rods, those 7 feet and over, are preferred by most catters, and offer the following advantages over short rods.

•*Increased casting distance.* This is important when bank fishing or angling in clear water. The best rods have a long handle and require two-handed casting, which is best for gently lob-casting a bait so it stays on the hook.

•*More "reach."* This lets you work rigs properly around cover or keep a feisty cat out of your prop.

•*Better control of your bait.* A long rod allows for accurate drifts and a natural presentation of your bait when stream fishing, by keeping more line off the water and out of the current.

•*More hook-setting and fighting power.* A long rod picks up slack line quicker and gives you extra leverage when battling trophy cats.

Although long rods are the trend these days, they are not mandatory. Short rods can also be used in many catfishing situations, but your odds of landing a trophy cat increase with a long rod.

COMPOSITION. The majority of fishing rod blanks are made of either fiberglass, graphite or combinations of the two. Fiberglass is more durable than graphite but lacks graphite's remarkable sensitivity. It is also heavier and bends more easily with the same amount of pull. Graphite is lighter and stiffer, and is more expensive than fiberglass. Graphite/fiberglass composites offer the best of both worlds – strength, sensitivity, flexibility and moderate pricing. They are probably the best choice for most cat fans.

If money is no object, consider the super-tough E-glass rods several companies sell. They're somewhat pricey but nearly indestructible, with extra strength for lifting, pulling and casting heavy rigs. A well-selected purchase can provide a lifetime of use.

QUALITY. Unfortunately for catfishermen on a budget, high quality and price go hand in hand. If a rod is inexpensive, it is probably made of cheap components and more likely to fail over many days of hard-core catting. Expensive rods are made of the best materials and components. The bottom line: don't lose the trophy of a lifetime due to the failure of a cheap rod. Listed below are some other features you might want to consider when purchasing a rod.

•*Long, reinforced fighting butts and blank-through-handle* construction provide superior strength and leverage for big-cat battles.

•*Black rods are almost invisible at night.* White and light-colored models are easier to see.

•*Rods* with glow-in-the-dark tips are very helpful for detecting night bites.

•*EVA foam handles* are less expensive and more durable than cork, but cork is more comfortable to grip.

Reels

Baitcasting, spinning or spin-casting reels?

Baitcasting reels are by far the most popular style for catfishing. They are toughest and provide more power for cranking in big fish. Look for a model with a solid frame, tough gears and a smooth drag, plus enough line capacity for the conditions you fish. The best ones hold at least 200 yards of 17- to 20-pound monofilament. For short-distance work, it's possible to load a baitcaster with heavier line than recommended and still get good performance, but don't push it or you can damage the reel's spindle.

Good baitcasting reels feature a "clicker" mechanism. The clicker gives an audible signal when line is pulled from the reel, thus indicating that a catfish is taking your bait. The clicker also keeps a soft, steady tension on the spool, preventing a cat from backlashing the reel when it runs with a bait. To use the clicker, simply push the free-spool button and engage the clicker switch.

Spinning reels have a place in catfishing, too. Their main applications are for long-distance casting and fishing light line (12-pound test and less). They also handle small baits better. If you want to have a good time catching cats, and won't be too upset if a monster snaps your line, traditional bass-fishing models work fine for most catfishing situations. If you're trying for a line-class record on light line, then opt for a well-balanced, long-rod/spinning reel combo matched precisely to your line size.

Spin-casting reels are still the traditional favorites of many catfish fans. None have the winching power or line capacity of a large baitcaster, but they offer simple push-button casting control with a soft delivery suitable for stinkbaits and small natural baits. This type of reel is perfect for children learning to cast, but don't expect it to hold up well when battling a hard-fighting trophy-class catfish.

Line

Catfish aren't line-shy, so you can use light or heavy line as situations dictate. Since most catfishing is done in and around cover, abrasion resistance is the most important factor to consider. Another is stretch. For catfishing, usually the less stretch, the better. There are several different categories of line used for catfishing; these include monofilament, the new "superlines" and braided nylon and Dacron®.

MONOFILAMENT. The monofilaments used by most anglers come in a bewildering array of colors, sizes and styles. The best mono for catfishing has low stretch and high abrasion resistance. Fortunately, most premium choices offer superb blends of tensile strength, limpness, abrasion resistance and knot strength. The best advice is to test several name brands and stick with those you know and trust. High-strength, small-diameter monofilaments testing 15 to 25 pounds are good inexpensive choices for all-round use, but when hunting the big boys, you may have to upgrade to 30-, 40-, or even 80-pound test.

Copolymer monofilament lines are another recent innovation. These are thin and soft with very little memory, yet they offer many times the abrasion resistance of monofilament, allowing them to be fished in the roughest cover without worry. They allow longer casting than most monos but also have more stretch. Available in 4- to 30-pound test, copolymers are now the favorite general-purpose lines for many catters.

SUPERLINES. These hi-tech, small-diameter lines are relatively new on the catfishing scene, but are becoming popular with some serious catmen. Most are made from Spectra® fibers, which is the same material used in body armor. Superlines come in two categories – braided and fused.

Braided types have the smallest diameter; for example, 50-pound test is the diameter of 10-pound mono. Braided superlines are also the most expensive.

Fused types are made by heat-fusing dozens of these fibers together. They are just as strong as the braided varieties, but their diameter is larger; 50-pound test has the diameter of 25-pound mono.

The advantages of using superlines are low stretch and small diameter. They have the lowest stretch of any other line type, which is great for sticking hooks into trophy cats, and the small diameter offers the least drag when fishing in heavy current. They are also waterproof, meaning they don't soak up water like braided Dacron. This is a bonus when fishing in cold weather because your hands won't get wet from the spray coming off the line when you cast. One final plus: these lines can be used over many seasons without deterioration.

Their main disadvantage is cost. Superlines can cost up to four times as much as a spool of monofilament. Overall, though, most catfishermen who use superlines feel the pluses outweigh the cost.

BRAIDED NYLON & DACRON. Some veteran catfishermen still spool their reels with braided nylon and Dacron line, or use them for leaders. These anglers contend that many of today's stiff, wiry lines can spook a cat by feel, but the softness of Dacron won't. The minimal stretch of Dacron also means good hook-setting power, superb sensitivity and more control when fighting a hefty fish. Braided nylon stretches more than Dacron and is not as popular as it once was with catfishermen.

Line visibility should also be considered before making a purchase. Dark-colored lines are considered a hindrance by many line-watching catfishermen, especially after dark. Experts use and recommend bright green, yellow and blue fluorescent monos that improve their ability to detect a bite.

At night, the violet glow of a black light greatly improves line visibility. However, fluorescent lines must be used for this to be effective. The blue and yellow monofilament lines made by most manufacturers work great for this.

Terminal Tackle

ooks, sinkers, bobbers and swivels are the basic components of catfishing rigs. To be a successful catfish angler, you must know how to select and assemble the proper terminal tackle.

Unfortunately, many anglers are confused by the seemingly endless variety of sizes and styles on today's market. Learn the differences so you can ideally equip yourself to handle any catfishing situation.

Hooks

These may be the least expensive item in your tackle box, but they also are the most important. The hook is the final link between fisherman and fish, and deserves the angler's utmost attention. There are two primary considerations when selecting a hook for catfishing – size and style.

Always use the smallest hook feasible. Small hooks penetrate quicker than big hooks. Small hooks also allow better bait presentations.

POPULAR HOOK STYLES include: (1) O'Shaughnessy, (2) Wide Gap, (3) Octopus, (4) Kirby and (5) Treble.

Small does not mean thin, however. The thin-wire hooks used by panfishermen straighten out when connected to even a modest-size catfish. Use heavy-wire designs sturdy enough to hold the fish you're after.

Match the size of hook to the type and size of bait. The hook point should remain exposed after impaling the bait. A hook that is too small often sets back into the bait on the hook set, failing to hook the fish.

Here are some general guidelines when determining hook size. When fishing night crawlers or catalpa worms for small catfish, you may need nothing larger than a size 2 or 1 hook. A 1/0 to 3/0 hook is good when presenting a small strip of thin cut-bait, but a 4/0 or 6/0 may be required when cut-bait is prepared in thick chunks. A 7/0 or 8/0 is necessary when using bluegills and other live baitfish up to 6 inches. Hooks up to 11/0 are necessary when using large baits in the 1-pound class.

Most catfishermen carry several different styles of hooks in their tackle box. The style is determined by the length of the hook shank, the bend and size of the eye, and the distance between the hook point and shank, or gap. The gap of a hook determines the size of bait that can be used. If the gap is too small, the hook point may not be fully exposed from the bait, meaning missed fish.

Each style of hook has a different function; the one you use depends on the size and type of bait being used. The O'Shaughnessy, for example, is an old-time favorite of many catters. It is an excellent, sturdy, multipurpose hook with a long shank, available in sizes up to 14/0. The Wide Gap hook is another favorite. Its open-gap design provides plenty of room for a large live bait or cut-bait. Other all-around hook styles include: The Octopus, which has an upturned eye and is good for lip-hooking live bait; Kirby, which has an offset point and a large eye that makes it easy to tie on heavy trotline cord; and Treble, which is one unit with three hooks and has multiple uses.

Because there are so many different kinds of baits and techniques used for catfishing, hook manufacturers have developed hooks specially designed for certain situations. On the following page are some specialty hooks used by catfishermen.

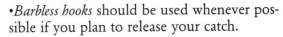

•*Barbless hooks* should be used whenever possible if you plan to release your catch.

•*Spring-wound treble hooks* are excellent for fishing doughbaits and other soft catfish baits.

•*Circle hooks* are popular with setliners. The point of this hook is perpendicular to its shaft. This design hooks a catfish in the corner of its mouth as it swims away with the bait and struggles against the tension of a trotline or limbline.

•*Liver or shad gut hooks* are double-hook rigs with a safety-pin design to hold the bait.

•*Double-needle hooks* have a special design that allows easier rigging of softshell crawfish and other live baits.

•*Baitholder* hooks have barbs sliced into the shank, which keeps bait from slipping off.

•*Weedless hooks* have a wire guard that keeps them from getting caught on weeds, logs and brush.

Sinkers

Because catfish are primarily bottom feeders, sinkers are a necessary part of most rigs. Carry plenty; you'll lose a lot to snags.

Sinkers are molded in many different sizes and shapes, but all serve one purpose – to carry bait down to where catfish are feeding. Choice depends primarily on the type of rig being fished, water depth, current velocity and bottom composition. Use a size that is just heavy enough to keep your bait in place.

Slip-sinkers slide freely on your line, usually above a barrel swivel or split shot used as a stop. Common styles include egg, bell, walking and bullet sinkers.

Egg, or barrel, sinkers (1) are the most popular sinker used by catfishermen. They have a hole through the middle and slide freely along the line. Their only drawback is they roll in strong current, often hanging on the bottom. They come in many sizes.

Bell sinkers (2), also called dipsey or bass-casting sinkers, are molded around a brass swivel. They are used for both slip-sinker and three-way rigs. The line is run through or tied to the swivel, which prevents line twist when drift-fishing or bouncing a bait across the bottom.

Walking sinkers (3) have a flattened "foot" shape and are used for casting or trolling bait along the bottom.

Bullet sinkers (4) have a cone shape that provides minimal drag and relative weedlessness. They are most often used when fishing soft plastic worms with dip baits. Some

---

SHARP hook points penetrate better and catch more fish than dull ones. When a point breaks or gets dull, you can simply tie on a new hook. But don't be misled into thinking a new hook is always a sharp hook. Cheap hooks are often made of soft, poor-quality steel and are poorly sharpened). Even new, high-quality hooks dull quickly when dragged through rocks or debris.

Examine your hook frequently to see if it needs sharpening. One simple method is to draw the hook's point across a fingernail. A sharp hook leaves a light scratch and digs into the nail. A

Sharp Anglers Use Sharp Hooks

dull hook "skates" across the nail without digging in. When necessary, touch up the point using a hook file.

Another option is to use "chemically sharpened" hooks. Many manufacturers offer a line of hooks made of a finer grade steel and then dipped in a chemical bath, which gives the hook a super-sharp point. These hooks can be twice as expensive as conventional hooks, but if you want sharp hooks out of the package, they are the best option.

The bottom line – make it a point to keep all your hooks needle sharp.

manufacturers make hollow brass bullet sinkers with internal beads that rattle for extra attraction.

Other sinker designs commonly used by cat men include bank, pyramid, split-shot, Bait-Walker™ bead-chain, rubber-core, and bottom-bouncer sinkers.

•*Bank sinkers* are molded entirely of lead, including the eye. They are mainly used on three-way rigs and are good in deep water.

•*Pyramid sinkers,* as the name suggests, are molded in a pyramid shape, with a lead or wire eye on the square end. They don't roll, so they hold bottom well where current or wave action are prevalent. Like bank and bell sinkers, they are frequently used to anchor three-way rigs.

•*The Bait-Walker™,* designed by midwestern river rat Dan Gapen, Sr., is relatively snagless and designed for fishing bait in fast river current.

•*Split shot* are versatile and convenient for light-tackle fishing when small amounts of weight are needed. They also are used to balance sliding floats, weight drift rigs and as makeshift sinker stops on bottom rigs.

•*Bottom-bouncers* are designed to "walk" across the bottom without snagging and are a common component of drift-fishing rigs. Most have a wire frame with a lead weight molded around the frame's arm.

Swivels

Catfish tend to twist and roll when hooked. So do many of the live baits used by catfish anglers. For this reason, many anglers add a swivel to their rigs. Swivels also serve as "stops" between slip-sinkers and hooks.

SWIVELS include (1) barrel, (2) ball-bearing, and (3) three-way.

Cheap snap swivels should be avoided. Instead, use top-quality barrel and ball-bearing swivels. Three-way swivels are an integral part of some catfish rigs, so keep a batch of those on hand as well.

BOBBERS. Whether you call them bobbers, floats or corks, these devices perform many functions important to catfish anglers. They add weight, making it easier to cast smaller baits; they hold your bait at a specific depth, indicate bites and let you fish your bait in hard-to-reach spots. A bobber also allows you to suspend a bait just off the bottom or over the top of submerged cover, meaning fewer snags.

Bobbers are made from hard plastic, foam, wood and cork. There are many styles from which to choose, and naturally, each has its strong points.

There are two types of bobbers – fixed and sliding. Fixed bobbers attach firmly to the line with spring-loaded hooks, pegs, rubber bands or other devices. They are best suited for fishing your bait no deeper than the length of your rod. This type is simple to set but often cumbersome to cast.

Sliding, or *slip*-bobbers have a hole through the middle and slide along the line, so you can reel the entire rig (bobber, sinker and hook) close to the rod tip. When cast, the bobber floats on its side while the sinker pulls the line through it. A knot or *bobber stop* on the line stops the rig at a preset depth, and the bobber stands up.

When selecting a bobber, take into account the size of bait and depth of the fish. You want one that both supports the bait and is easy to see. Keep several different styles and sizes in your tackle box to match different fishing conditions.

Specialty bobbers, such as night bobbers and European-style floats are gaining popularity with catfishermen.

Night bobbers have a light on top that is powered by a cyalume stick or tiny lithium battery, depending on the brand. They're super for catfishing after dark.

European-style floats come in numerous styles that are designed for a variety of fishing conditions, many of which involve current. They are made of balsa wood and when properly weighted are supersensitive. In still water, for example, the biggest fish often pick up the bait so the float "rises" up through the water rather than sinking. This kind of take is often hard to detect with most American bobbers.

Shape of the bobber depends on function. "Fat" ones float more shot where you need longer casts or where current is

Tying a Stop Knot for Slip-Bobber Fishing

THE SLIP-BOBBER FISHERMAN stops his float from running up the line by tying a stop knot. This knot moves readily through the rod guides and cinches tight enough so it won't slide up and down the line. These knots can be purchased pre-tied from a tackle store, but with practice, you can tie them easily on your own.

To tie this knot, start with a 6-inch piece of 10- to 15-pound nylon or Dacron line, and lay it alongside the main line. Make a loop in the short line. Wrap the end of the short line through the loop and around the main line four or five times. Pull on the ends of the short line to cinch up the knot; trim the tag ends. Add a small bead and your slip-bobber, and you're ready to go.

strong – in tailwaters, for example. "Antenna" styles with elongated tops work best in still or slowly moving water, and with lighter baits. When a fish takes with an antenna float, you can see where it moves by the tilt of the antenna top. European floats are some of the most sensitive fishing floats ever devised, and every catfish angler would be wise to try them out.

One final word about bobbers: whenever possible, select one that is easy to see. Bright, fluorescent colors stand out on rippled water surfaces much better than white or cork-colored bobbers. If you're fishing clear, shallow water, or if fish seem fussy, you may want to use a transparent plastic bobber. Under most conditions, though, bright-colored models are best.

Catfishing Rigs

The best catfishing rigs usually are the simplest. With fewer components, there's less chance something will fail. Simple rigs also are easier to make and easier to cast, plus there's less weight to interfere with natural-looking bait presentations.

The simplest rig of all is nothing more than a baited hook at the end of your line. It works well in a surprising variety of catfishing situations. Most of the time, though, you'll have to use a weight to get your bait on or near the bottom. In fact, rigs with weights as heavy as 16 ounces are used by catfishermen at certain times.

The following section illustrates the most common bottom and float rigs used by catfishermen, as well as some variations for special situations.

Bottom Rigs

Since most catfish are found on or near the bottom, bottom-fishing rigs are by far the most common used by catfishermen. These can be put into two categories: slip-sinker rigs and fixed-sinker rigs.

SLIP-SINKER RIGS. These are favored by many catfishermen, because they allow the fish to run with a bait without feeling any tension. The simplest slip-sinker rig consists of a hook, an egg sinker, and a split shot for a stop (below). To improve on this rig, add a swivel between the sinker and the hook. By substituting a bell or walking sinker for the egg sinker, you create a rig less likely to roll along the bottom and snag when fishing

in current. You can dis-
pense with the swivel altogether and let the sinker
ride snug against the baited
hook. Few catfishermen use
this simplified version, but
it works great in heavy
current where a long
leader is likely to get
snagged.

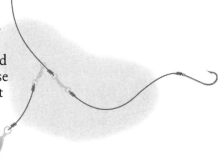

Another variation of a slip-sinker rig involves adding an
additional swivel above the main-line swivel, then adding
a 6-inch dropper line and a bell or bank sinker (above).
English fishermen refer to this as a *paternoster rig;* it allows
the bait to ride higher off the bottom than an in-line rig.

FIXED-SINKER RIGS. With these rigs, your bait rides
higher than it would with a slip rig. They also anchor your
bait better in strong current and are popular with catfishermen who fish tailrace waters. This is a versatile presentation, useful for both still-fishing and drift-fishing.

The *three-way rig* (below), also called the Wolf River rig in
some parts of the country, is

probably the most popular
of this style. To make this rig,
tie the main line to one eye of a
three-way swivel, and add drop lines 12 and 24 inches long
to the other two eyes. Tie a hook to the longer drop line
and a sinker (bell, pyramid or bank) to the other. If you
fish in very snaggy conditions, the sinker drop line should
be a lighter pound test than the main line. This way, if the
sinker gets hung up, the lighter dropper line breaks, and
you can salvage the rest of the rig. If a three-way swivel is
unavailable, use a barrel swivel instead. Tie the main line
to one eye and the two drop lines to the other.

A fixed-sinker rig that works well for small cats and bullheads involves placing the hook in front of the sinker so that light bites can be detected better. This is called the *dropper loop rig* (left). To make this rig, simply tie a bell or bank sinker to the end of your line, then tie in a dropper loop knot (p. 97) 12 to 18 inches in front of the sinker. Then add a 6-inch section of line with a hook to the loop. In areas without hook restrictions, you can add multiple loops and hooks farther up the line.

Drift rigs, those commonly used by steelhead fishermen, are good catfish rigs in certain situations, such as in small streams with light current, or when drift-fishing relatively shallow water. To make this rig, simply tie on a hook, and add split shot 12 to 18 inches up the line (below). In snaggy areas, modify this rig by adding a barrel swivel, then attach a 6-inch dropper to one of the eyes. Add the appropriate amount of split shot to the dropper. If the shot gets hung up, apply pressure and the shot pulls off the dropper, saving the hook and swivel.

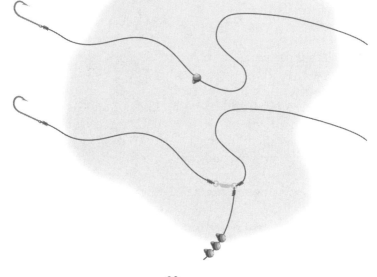

Float Rigs

Float rigs are great for drifting baits through river cat hide-outs, or targeting suspended catfish. The simplest consist of nothing more than a fixed bobber above a hook and perhaps a split shot or two. A more versatile version employs a slip-bobber (below, far right). Tie a bobber stop (p. 89) on the line, then add a bead and a slip-bobber. Attach a hook and add two or three split shot to sink the bait and stand up the slip-bobber. Adjust the stop knot so the slip-bobber suspends the bait at the desired depth. With this rig, the bobber slips down to the split shot to allow casting, then slips up to the bobber stop to hold the bait at the correct depth.

A variation of this rig (right) performs well when fishing large live baitfish for flatheads, or big pieces of cut-bait for blue and channel cats. Affix the bobber stop, then run a bead, slip-bobber and an egg sinker up the line. You'll need a big float to hold up this rig. The size of the sinker is determined by the size of the bait. Big baits require heavy sinkers, often up to 4 or 5 ounces for a sizable bluegill or sucker.

Tie a barrel swivel beneath the sinker, at the end of the main line. Then, to the bottom eye of the swivel, affix a 10- to 20-inch leader and a large hook. For flatheads, impale a large baitfish just behind the dorsal fin. For large blues and channels, use a large chunk of cut-bait, such as shad or skipjack herring.

Specialty Rigs

Creative catfishermen have come up with countless variations of standard cat rigs. Of course, they can't all be shown, but below are some of the well-known specialty rigs that have produced more than just a few nice cats.

Take the paternoster rig mentioned in the slip-sinker section, add a slip-bobber, and you have a *float-paternoster rig* (left). This rig works great for fishing a large live bait in shallow water. Slide a slip-bobber on the line before tying the rig. The sinker lies on the bottom while the baitfish struggles against the float. Leave a foot or two of slack line between the sinker and the float; this gives the bait extra room to think it's escaping. The dropper line to the sinker should be light enough to break off if the sinker gets snagged.

Bait-Walkers and *bottom bouncers* are thought of by many fishermen as walleye rigs, but they have applications to

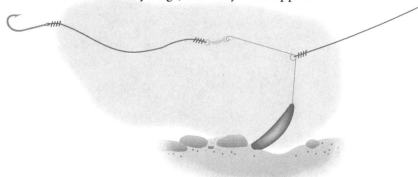

catfishing as well. Simply attach a leader of 12 to 36 inches to the eye of the swivel, and add a hook. Bait-Walkers (opposite, bottom) can be fished in fast current. The foot of the sinker is virtually snag-free, and the safety-pin shape keeps the bait near the bottom. This rig works best when cast directly downstream.

Bottom bouncers (below) are a similar design, but the wire continues through the weight, which causes the sinker to ride up and over snags. Bottom bouncers are great for drift-fishing live or cut-bait over snaggy areas where other sinkers would surely hang. To rig, tie the main line to the front eye, and attach the leader to the swivel on top.

QUICK TIPS:

• ADD a plastic bead to the main line between the sinker and swivel to protect the knot connection.

• USE a floating jig head to suspend small baits off the bottom. The hook is molded into the head.

• ATTACH a fixed bobber just above the hook to suspend a large bait off the bottom.

Knots

Most catfish anglers need to know only two or three basic knots. Here are some of the most useful.

Improved Clinch Knot. This is a basic knot everyone should learn for tying leaders and lines to hooks and swivels. The knot is dependable, easy to tie and retains nearly 100 percent of line strength.

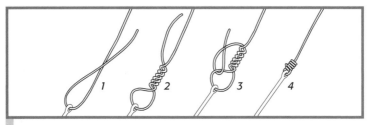

(1) Pass end of the line through eye of hook or swivel. (2) Pull about 6 inches of line through and double it back against itself. Twist five to seven times. (3) Pass end of the line through the small loop formed just above the eye, then through the big loop just created. Be careful coils don't overlap. (4) Pull tag end and main line so that coiled line tightens against the eye. Again, be careful coils haven't overlapped. Trim excess.

Palomar Knot. This is another basic knot that provides almost 100 percent of line strength. It is easy and fast to tie and handy for attaching hooks, swivels and eyed sinkers on terminal tackle rigs or trotline stagings. This is very popular with catmen because it is easily tied at night with a minimum of practice.

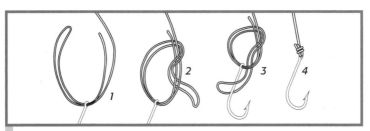

(1) Double about 6 inches of line and pass through the eye of the hook. (2) Tie a simple overhand knot in the doubled line, letting the hook hang loose. Avoid twisting the lines. (3) Pull the end of the loop down, passing it completely over the hook. (4) Pull both ends of the line to draw up the knot.

Dropper Loop Knot. This knot provides a handy attachment point for a dropper line when fishing with several hooks.

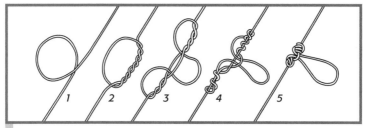

(1) Form a loop in the line, and wrap the end overhand seven times through the loop. (2) Keep open the midpoint where the turns, or twists, are being made. A pencil inserted in the middle turn helps keep the strands separated so this can be done easily. (3) Hold the other side of the loop and pull it through the opening. Stick your finger through the loop so it does not pull back through. (4) Hold the loop with your teeth, and pull gently on both ends of the line, making the turns gather and pack down on either side of the loop. (5) Tighten with a hard pull on both ends of the line.

Accessories

atfishermen need little in the way of tackle and accessories. Need and want are two different things, however. You'll certainly want a variety of accessories to make your catfishing junkets more comfortable and productive. Here are some to consider.

ELECTRONICS

Serious catfish anglers want to know what's underwater in the way of structure and cover where catfish lurk, as well as where the catfish themselves are. This is why sonar devices are important to catfishermen.

Sonar units send out sound waves that are reflected back to a device called a transducer by anything dense enough to reflect them, be it a catfish, a school of shad or a snag on the bottom. The unit then displays a signal showing what's down there.

There are three types of depth finders: flashers, LCR's and color videos, all of which work on the same basic principle. The main difference is in the way they display readings. Catfishermen need only concern themselves with the first two, though, as color videos are quite expensive and a bit of overkill for catfishing.

Flashers display the reading on a dial or bar, and the reading is instantaneous, showing bottom readings at high speed. A suspended fish usually shows as a strong line, or "blip," on the dial.

Liquid Crystal Recorders, or LCR's, show the reading on a screen made of small squares, called *pixels.* The higher the pixel count, the better the picture. These screens are slower than a flasher, and oftentimes you'll be over structure, such as a hump, before it shows on the screen. LCR's, especially high-end models, are better than flashers at distinguishing fish from other objects. Fish appear as small boomerangs, or "hooks," on the screen.

Since a depth finder is cheaper than scuba gear, serious catfishermen should own one. Prices are much more reasonable than they were in the past, and the displays require less interpretation. Check out the many models available, and settle on one that best serves your needs and budget. Without sonar, you're fishing blind, especially on big water. With it, you can see what's underwater, which definitely increases your odds of catching fish.

Another electronic device that big-water catfishermen might want to consider using is a GPS (Global Positioning System). These units receive satellite signals that give your location. For example, if you find a small catfish hump in the middle of a big reservoir, simply save the location (called a *waypoint*). The next time you return, call up that waypoint and the GPS unit will guide you to it.

LANDING NETS

You can land small cats by hoisting them topside with your fishing line or your hands. But if you're after trophy cats, always carry a big, sturdy landing net. The best have a large reinforced hoop, long handle (at least 48") and a long net (48" or more) made from soft small-mesh netting (to keep from injuring a catfish's fragile skin).

QUICK TIP: After netting a big cat, lift the net by the hoop and not the handle.

TACKLE BOXES

Selection of a tackle box is mostly a matter of personal preference. One excellent type to consider consists of an outer waterproof Cordura® bag with several large storage pockets. Inside are several multicompartmented plastic boxes with adjustable dividers. By moving the dividers, you can customize your storage area to properly arrange the hooks, sinkers, swivels and other tackle inside. The pockets on the outer bag can be used to store larger items such as fishing line, pliers, a stringer and so forth. Hard plastic models with a large cavity on top are great for carrying tubs of stinkbait. Some manufacturers are making boxes with a tight-sealing O-ring to keep the smell of odoriferous commercial baits inside.

ROD HOLDERS

There are two kinds of rod holders – those you mount on your boat and those you stick in the soil when bankfishing. In both cases, it's best to buy top-quality brands. A big catfish can yank a poorly made rod holder into the drink before you have time to react.

Rod holders for your boat should mount securely with no chance of slippage. Bankfishing models have long sturdy spikes at the bottom to permit secure upright placement. Good ones of both varieties allow for quick, easy rod-angle adjustments. Also, be sure the holders you purchase are big enough to properly accommodate the large rod butts and handles of catfish rods.

SHAD-COLLECTING GEAR

Many cat men use shad for bait. Cast nets often are used to collect them. These are sized in feet. For example, a 6-foot cast net has a radius of 6 feet. When thrown, it opens into a circle 12 feet in diameter. A beginner should start with a smaller diameter cast net; the larger ones are harder to throw. They do, however, catch more shad with each throw. A 5- or 6-footer with 3/8-inch mesh is fine for the weekend angler.

QUICK TIP: Gear for collecting shad includes: cast net; round, battery-powered aerated bait well; dip net; small cooler with ice for dead bait and shad-saver chemical.

Once collected, shad must be properly stored. If you intend to use them for cut-bait, simply throw them on ice in a cooler. To keep them alive, use a round aerated bait tank that holds at least 20 gallons of water. To reduce losses, add a water con-ditioner that removes ammonia and surface foam, things that make these baitfish hard to keep alive. A bait net for retrieving shad from the tank completes the setup.

TROTLINING GEAR

A simple homemade trotline can be created with only a few items. The main line is constructed of 600-pound-test nylon cord. The stagings or trots (drop lines) are made from 100- to 200-pound-test nylon cord. Hardware includes bar-rel swivels with large eyes, and hooks – usually Limerick, O'Shaughnessy, or circle style in sizes 2/0 to 6/0. Trotline brads are also useful. These are clamped on the main line to prevent stagings from sliding.

For safety's sake, some cat men are using specially made trotline clips. Drop lines are attached to a trotline clip instead of the main line. The stainless steel clips snap on and off the trotline. Squeeze the clip to remove it, and bring the catfish and hook into the boat for safe handling.

JUG-FISHING GEAR

To make jug-fishing rigs, all you need are some empty plas-tic jugs, some line, sinkers and hooks. Empty milk or soda jugs in quart, 1-liter or 2-liter sizes are ideal. Dacron line in 50- to 100-pound test makes drop lines that are easily wound around the jugs for storage. Monofilament can be used but has a tendency to get loopy and hard to handle. Rubbercore sinkers slide easily on the drop lines and stay in place better than other styles. One-half- to 2-ounce sizes are most often used, depending on current velocity. Any hook style is OK, but circle hooks give better hook sets with jug lines. The hooks' size should be geared toward the size fish you're targeting. One manufacturer offers a unique plastic jug-fishing spool that has two threaded col-lars. Screw an empty 2-liter soda bottle into each collar. The bottles now lie in a V-shaped configuration with the spool at the point of the V. Add line, a hook and sinker, and you're ready to fish. The spool's off-axis placement prevents line from unwinding when a fish pulls. When a cat strikes, the unit tips up.

OTHER GEAR

Needlenose pliers are among the cat man's most important tools. Use them to remove hooks, cut line and dozens of other tasks.

Many catfishermen, however, now carry multiple-use tools. These handy items usually feature a needlenose pliers, knife, file and numerous other helpful tools.

You'll also want a good set of wide-jawed skinning pliers. Veteran catfishermen prefer stainless steel models with nonslip handles.

Other items to consider having include: boat anchor(s); lawn chair or stool; ice chest; drift sock(s), for drift-fishing; sharp knife and cutting board, for preparing cutbait; spotlights, lanterns, headlamps and other night lights, for navigating, rigging and finding setlines after dark; gear bag, to hold lots of small accessories; hand towel and soap, since catfishing can be messy; insect repellent; quality stringer, to keep fish alive if you don't have a live well; brush clamp, for securing a boat to shoreline trees; fluorescent tape, for marking trot- and limblines; leather and/or rubber gloves to keep hands from getting cut up in the maw of big cats; marker buoy, to pinpoint good catfish spots; weighing scale; and rod bells and electronic strike indicators, to signal bites after dark.

Natural Baits

To catch catfish consistently, be selective about the bait you use. Some are better than others. Choosing the best bait from the vast array available is perplexing for novice catters. But with some homework, that task doesn't have to be so intimidating. By understanding each species' food preferences and habits, you can narrow the choices to a select few.

First, determine what catfish feed on in the body of water you'll fish. Local fisheries biologists, bait shops and anglers can help in this regard, so seek their advice. As a rule, the most abundant forage in a body of water is also the best to use as bait.

It is important to match the type of bait to the species of catfish you're after. For example, if trophy flatheads are your goal, using catalpa worms isn't wise. Small flatheads love them, but they're not on a big flathead's menu. Large, live bait is the key to success here.

If you want a few channel cats for the frying pan, your bait selection can run the gamut from nightcrawlers to crayfish. But to catch a heavyweight river blue, you'd be smarter to use a good-sized chunk of shad or skipjack herring.

Another tip: Examine the stomach contents of catfish you've already caught. If most have shad in their bellies, then shad are an excellent bait. If their tummies are round with crayfish, use crayfish, if possible. Let's look at some baits, conventional and unconventional, that can put catfish in your boat.

SHAD & HERRING

These oily baitfish are abundant in most catfish waters, and consequently make excellent baits. Whether they're used live or dead, cut or whole, shad and herring are the bait of choice of many catfishermen. Large blue cats feed primarily on these baitfish. Trophy channel cats and flatheads are regularly taken on them, too.

In some areas, fresh shad and herring can be purchased from bait dealers, but in most cases, you'll have to catch your own. Check local regulations to determine legal methods.

Using a cast net is the most effective method for catching shad. Many anglers hang lights over the water after dark to draw schools of these baitfish into a small area. In many locales, however, they are so abundant this isn't necessary. A couple of throws with a cast net brings in enough for a day's fishing. Look for shad around dam tailwaters, bridges, piers and riprap. Skipjack herring, when present, are caught in these same areas on ultralight tackle using 1/64- or 1/32-ounce lead-head jigs.

Shad and herring are sensitive and die easily. To keep shad alive, store them uncrowded in highly oxygenated water. Use a large, round, well-insulated, aerated tank with cool water, or rig a perforated garbage can to carry them alongside your boat. A gallon of water supports about four large baitfish. Make sure to remove all dead shad and keep on ice; they spoil fast.

Skipjack herring, on the other hand, cannot be kept alive for any length of time. It is best to catch them fresh and immediately put them on ice.

Always use fresh shad and herring. Hook live fish through the back, lips, nostrils or eyes.

OTHER FISH

Big catfish, especially flatheads, prefer live fish over most other natural baits. Consequently, anything one pound and under with fins is fair game for these predators, and also works well as bait.

Live sunfish, where legal, are hot catfish baits, especially for large flatheads. Fish up to 8 inches are used, usually hooked behind the dorsal fin. Suckers and creek chubs, 6 to 12 inches long, freshly seined or caught from a creek or river, also make great catfish bait because they're active. These are also available at many bait shops. Other fish that make good cat baits include small carp, mooneyes, goldeyes, alewifes, killifish, madtoms and stonecats. Among "bait-store" baits, goldfish, fathead minnows and large golden shiners are hard to beat. Ciscoes are also a great cat bait,

HOW TO THROW A CAST NET

Cast nets provide the best means for catching shad, but throwing one properly requires lots of practice. The photos below demonstrate the proper way to throw one.

TIE the retrieving line of the net to your wrist, and with the same hand, grasp the net where it is attached to the line.

HOLD the weighted line with the other hand and your teeth. Twisting like a discus thrower, hoist the net into the water. The net should open into a big circle, and the weights pull it down to surround the fish.

PULL the line to draw the net shut and retrieve the baitfish.

but the only way to get them is from a bait shop in a frozen form.

The attractiveness of these baits can be improved by snipping off a couple of fins or a portion of the tail. The combination of the fish struggling and the fresh blood flowing from the wounds attracts catfish. These fish can be hooked either through the lips or behind the back dorsal fin.

Most of these fish, especially the soft-rayed ones, such as goldeyes, ciscoes, suckers and alewives, make great fresh cut bait as well.

BULLHEADS

Perhaps the best bait for big flatheads is also the most surprising. Bullheads are a favorite target of flatheads in waters where both are common. They've been used as bait by flathead fans since at least the 19th century.

In his 1953 book, *Catfishin'*, Joe Mathers called bullheads "excellent, especially for large catfish."

"Use small living forms, 3 to 6 inches long," he wrote. "Snip off the barbels, spines and dorsal fin causing the fish to bleed and flounder in the water. They are very tough, easy to keep alive and excellent for use on trot or other set lines. Small bullheads usually can be taken in great numbers with a seine or on hook and line from backwaters, bayous, ponds and small lakes and streams . . ." Be sure to check local regulations to determine if there are any restrictions on collecting or using them for bait.

HOOK a bullhead behind the adipose fin for best results; snip the pectoral spines to increase its effectiveness.

WORMS

Nightcrawlers and other earthworms are probably the number-one bait used by the average catfisherman. They are one of the easiest baits to catch and keep, and are ideal for catching small, eating-size catfish and bullheads.

Nightcrawlers and worms are available at virtually every bait shop across the country. You can gather your own by raking through damp leaves in flower beds and woods, digging them in a garden with a pitchfork, or picking them from your yard in the evening after a good, soaking rain.

Like most baits, worms must be kept cool to stay alive. Keep them in a cooler at all times when in the boat; once they heat up, they spoil fast. To keep worms alive between fishing trips, store them either in your refrigerator or in a container of moist leaves and dirt in the basement or another cool place.

The secret to catching cats on worms is generosity. Don't use just one worm or a piece of a worm, or catfish may miss it. Gob two to four plump worms on your hook, and mash a few pieces so body juices flow into the water. If catfish are in the neighborhood, they'll home in on the scent trail, and you won't have to wait long for action.

Another tip: use a hypodermic syringe or special-made worm blower to inflate the worms. A shot of air in the body lifts the worms up, keeps them off the bottom, and makes them more visible to catfish.

CRAYFISH

Whether you call them crawfish, crawdads or crayfish, these crustaceans are a dynamite catfish bait. In many lakes, ponds and streams, they are the primary forage of channel cats, bullheads, small flatheads and small blues. They also are illegal to transport in some states, so check your regulations.

Some bait shops carry crayfish, but most of the time you'll have to find your own. Collect them by turning rocks on a stream bottom and grabbing them with your hands, a dip net or a seine. Crayfish traps baited with fish parts in a cheesecloth bag also work. Keep crayfish in a minnow bucket with wet leaves or moss in the bottom.

The best crayfish are "peelers," those that have molted their hard outer shell, and are soft to the touch. Small- to medium-size hardshells also work, but break off their pincers to keep them from grabbing objects on the bottom.

To mimic their natural action, rig them for a backward retrieve. Thread the hook up, through and out the top of the tail, and work them across the bottom with a slow, stop-and-go motion. A broken-off tail or piece of peeled tail meat also works.

MUSSELS

Big blue and channel cats often feed on mussels or "freshwater clams." The inch-long exotic Asiatic clam *(Corbicula)*, now common in many southern lakes and rivers, is a special favorite for catfish, but native mussels – especially smaller varieties like lilliputs, wartybacks and deertoes – are also eaten. The bellies of some smaller cats sometimes are stuffed with tiny zebra mussels, the noxious invader that has colonized many waters. Large cats sometimes swallow large mussels that may be 8 inches long and as big around as a man's wrist.

Shell and all is eaten by the catfish, regardless of the mussel species. Digestive juices kill the mussel, the shell opens, the flesh inside is digested and then the shell is passed by the fish. At times, catfish literally rattle from all the shells in their gut.

Gather your own mussels using a dip net or by feeling for them in mud or sand bottom in shoreline shallows. (Be cautious during your collecting, however. Many species of mussels are protected under the Endangered Species Act. Check with your state wildlife agency to determine what's legal.) If there's a shelling industry along your river, visit a local sheller to get a bucket of flesh after he's steamed the mussels and separated shell from flesh.

To fish with mussels, remove the flesh from the shell and use it fresh. You can also allow the meat to sour for a day or two in an open container with plenty of "clam juice" covering it. You may have to tie the meat to the hook shank with sewing thread to keep it from coming off.

CATALPA WORMS

Found mostly in the southern United States, this worm is the caterpillar of the catalpa sphinx moth, a pretty little nocturnal insect few people ever see in its adult form. In spring, female moths lay thousands of eggs in clusters on the undersides of catalpa tree leaves. Ten to 14 days later, the eggs hatch into tiny caterpillars with a whale of an appetite for catalpa leaves.

The velvety larvae grow quickly and are soon one to three inches long and as big around as a pencil. They're black, yellow and white in color, and have a wicked-looking but harmless spine on their rear end.

Fishermen gather catalpa worms from April to June, depending on the latitude in which they live. Most non-anglers are eager to get rid of them, but be sure to ask permission before you start collecting.

Once you have permission, gathering catalpa worms is simple. Those on low branches can be picked from the leaves. For those higher up, place a white sheet on the ground under the tree, and use a long cane pole to slap the leaves. This produces a shower of falling worms. Once grounded, they are easy to find and pick off the sheet. Store them in a cool container with a few catalpa leaves.

To fish catalpa worms, thread one on a fine wire hook, leaving a bit of worm hanging free on each end. Some fishermen believe this bait works even better with the worm turned inside out on the hook.

The worms spit a brown fluid that stains your hands, but this is simply plant juice, the worms' way of discouraging predators. The liquid is harmless.

Trotliners are especially fond of catalpa worms because it's easy to gather large numbers quickly and inexpensively. They are tough and elastic, making them difficult for a catfish to pull off a hook, another favorable characteristic.

Catalpa worms are only available during a few months each year, but you can easily store them for later use. Catfish take them live or dead. To store the worms, drop them in a container of ice water to retain their color. Then put 20 to 25 of them in a quart-size zip-seal bag and fill with corn meal. Place the bag in the freezer, and pull it out again when you're ready to fish.

FROGS, TOADS & SALAMANDERS

Although rarely used by today's cat men, amphibians are excellent baits for big and small catfish alike. The best frogs include leopard, green, pickerel and bullfrogs. Small toads are also a surprisingly good bait. Salamanders make excellent cat bait, especially large larval forms and aquatic species like mudpuppies, sirens and amphiumas (Congo eels). Waterdogs, the larval form of the tiger salamander, are raised commercially and sold by many bait dealers.

Some bait shops sell frogs, but you can also catch them by hand. The easiest way to catch frogs and toads is to drive a rural road on a warm, rainy, spring night. Pick an area where traffic volume is low, and take a friend along. When the quarry is spotted, the passenger hops out, catches it and places it in a minnow bucket with a lid to which a little water has been added. It's possible to gather dozens of frogs and toads this way on a single night.

Live frogs are best used as surface or mid-water baits on limblines, bobby poles and surface trotlines. Freshly killed frogs cut in two or more pieces are also good bottom baits. Small toads are usually more active surface baits than frogs, because they continually struggle to reach the bank.

Hook frogs, toads and salamanders through both lips or in the thick part of one hind leg. No sinker should be added that might inhibit the bait's natural action. A live amphibian struggling at the surface is a morsel few catfish can resist. Check local regulations for restrictions on their use.

LEECHES

Regarded primarily as a walleye bait in the Midwest, these little creatures are also an excellent cat bait. They are tough and stay on hooks very well. Not known as a trophy cat bait, leeches are ideal for catching eating-size catfish.

In north-central states, they're readily available from bait dealers, but elsewhere you'll have to collect your own. Ponds with lush growths of cattails and lily pads are good places to catch them. To do this, put fresh beef liver in a burlap sack and toss it into shallow water. Leeches squirm through the fabric to reach the bait.

Store leeches in cool water in a minnow bucket or Styrofoam® cooler. Check them every couple of days and discard any that are dead or sluggish. The best leeches are ribbon leeches, which squirm actively when held. Avoid large horse leeches, which are soft and lifeless when held. Horse leeches are rarely eaten by any fish.

CUT-BAITS

Pieces or chunks of sliced baitfish are excellent baits for catfish, especially for blues and channels. Body fluids from these baits attract cats from long distances. Oily baitfishes work best – shad, herring, ciscoes, etc. – but when these aren't available, almost any baitfish works.

Cut-bait is prepared many ways. Some anglers fillet strips from the sides or belly of the fish, saving the carcass and entrails for later use. Others cut the bait in chunks. Vary what you use until you determine what catfish want. If fillets don't work, try using heads or tails. If these don't work, try other pieces.

Match the bait's size to the fish you're likely to catch. In waters with few cats over 5 or 6 pounds, use small chunks or strips of cut-bait. Where bigger cats are common, 4- to 6-inch-long baits aren't out of place.

When using fillets for bait, leave the skin on, then thread the fillet on the hook. For chunk bait or "steaks," slice crosswise through the fish, and divide it into head, midsection and tail pieces, or just head and tail. Hook the head through the eyes or mouth. When using tail or body pieces, run the hook completely through, then turn it down and run it back through again, leaving the point exposed.

The best cut-bait is fresh. Baitfish that are freshly killed or have died the night before and have been kept on ice far outperform bait that is days or even weeks old. Also, when fishing with cut-bait, re-bait frequently. The juices that attract catfish wash out quickly, so keep a fresh piece on at all times.

Commercial Baits

I f you're a serious catter, some day you'll go home reeking of stinkbait. Catfish love stinkbait like kids love candy, and every dedicated catter has his favorite version – a malodorous brew of blood, guts, cheese, rotten fish and who knows what – he swears is head and shoulders above the rest. There are more stinkbait recipes than you can possibly imagine.

Commercial baits cover a wide array of bait considered "stinkbaits," including blood bait, dip baits, sponge baits, tube baits, doughbaits and chunk baits in a zillion varieties. All catch cats, but only if you understand the advantages and disadvantages of each.

Don't plan on catching lots of trophy cats using these baits. Small channel and blue cats are most likely to be caught on stinkbaits. Young fish of these species scavenge more than heavyweight adults. As they grow in size, their diet becomes less varied, consisting mostly of live baitfish, crayfish and other abundant forage. Flathead catfish feed almost exclusively on live fish. Because they scavenge very little, stinkbaits rarely catch them.

BLOOD BAIT

Catfish are readily attracted to blood, and catters have long made blood bait to tempt channel cats, small blue cats and bullheads. Almost any mammal or bird blood works and can be obtained at little cost from meat processing plants.

Blood bait's main advantage is its tremendous "cat appeal." Blood attracts catfish quickly over long distances. It also keeps indefinitely when frozen. Bait can be thawed and refrozen each trip until it's gone.

Blood bait's most serious drawback is poor hookability. It just won't stay on the hook. To overcome this problem, wrap the blood bait in a small square of nylon stocking, pull the four corners together, then thread the hook through the corners, leaving the point uncovered. Without the stocking cover, casting blood bait is virtually impossible, and even slight currents force constant rebaiting.

Blood bait is also extremely messy, so have a towel handy to keep clean when baiting hooks.

Fortunately, blood bait's disadvantages are largely outweighed by its great cat appeal. For finicky cats in quiet water, few baits work better.

> QUICK TIP: How to Make and Use Blood Bait.
>
> •Make your own blood bait by pouring ½ inch of blood in a shallow pan. Refrigerate until the blood coagulates.
>
> •Cut the thickened blood into small chunks and store in a plastic container or resealable plastic bag.
>
> •Pinch off a piece when needed and thread on a hook, or wrap in a square of nylon mesh.

DOUGHBAITS

These are probably the most prevalent version of stinkbait sold today. Most have the consistency of modeling clay and are stored in plastic tubs or glass jars. All of them smell to high heaven.

Most doughbaits are effective cat-catchers, but beware of poor-quality products prolific in bait shops. Test several brands before settling on one.

Cat appeal is the most important quality of any stinkbait, and fortunately, this trait isn't hard to find in commercial doughbaits. The downside of such baits is hookability. Many doughbaits are practically useless, because they won't stay hooked when casting, especially during hot weather. Cloth doughbait bags and spring-wound bait-holder treble hooks are helpful. The best doughbaits can be molded around a regular hook to form a firm ball that won't fly off when casting. During really hot weather, keep doughbaits in a cooler to keep the mixture firm and easier to mold on the hook.

To properly fish doughbaits, don't move the bait too often. Give careful consideration to locating likely catfishing hot spots, then, once you cast, don't move your bait for 15 to 20 minutes. Doughbait must melt to lay a scent trail. If there are no nibbles in the specified time, then relocate.

Although there are plenty of commercial doughbaits, it's fun to make your own. One simple method is to mix flour and water to form a pasty dough. Add your favorite flavoring – anise oil, commercial catfish scents, rotten fish, blood, rancid cheese, etc. – then roll the dough into balls and store in a sealed container.

"Grocery Store" Baits

AS THEIR NAME IMPLIES, grocery store baits can be purchased at your local supermarket. Among those commonly used are fresh and frozen shrimp, cheese, hot dogs, moist chunk-style dog food, bread and bars of Ivory soap, an unusual yet productive bait that's been popular with cat men for many years.

Chicken liver, the most popular of these baits, is a favorite of channel cats, bullheads, and, occasionally, small blues and flatheads. Cats quickly zero in on the scent and taste of poultry blood trailing from the tissue. Turkey, pork and beef liver are recommended by some catters, but most catfishermen agree that none seems to work as well as chicken liver.

Some catters prefer fresh livers; others prefer frozen. Either way, you'll have difficulty keeping the bait on a hook unless you first wrap it in a piece of cheesecloth or nylon stocking. Lay a small piece of liver on a square of material, pull up the four corners, then run a hook through the corners, leaving the barb exposed. This keeps the liver from flying off when you cast, and in no way affects its cat-attracting qualities. Some hook manufacturers make a special safety-pin style hook (p. 85) to keep the piece of liver in place.

If you go catfishing often, you can buy chicken liver very inexpensively in bulk and keep a supply on hand in your freezer.

DIP BAITS

Dip baits are packaged in jars or tubs like doughbaits but have a slightly thinner consistency. (Be sure to read the label so you know which you are buying.) Because they won't cling to a hook, they're fished using a special lure called a "catfish worm," a short, thick plastic grub with rings or dimples to hold the dip bait, with a snelled hook buried in the tail.

To rig for dip bait fishing, tie a catfish worm on your line below a slip sinker, then dip it in bait and push it around with a stick until thoroughly covered. Be sure bait is forced into the worm's pores or grooves. Cast the lure, let it fall to the bottom, then wait until a catfish homes in on the scent.

Dip bait's main advantage is cleanliness. Properly done, you never touch the bait. Additionally, steel-shy cats drop the soft worm less than they drop bait-covered hooks.

The primary disadvantage of dip bait fishing is keeping bait on your worm. Dip baits melt quickly, so you must dunk your lure rather frequently. Catfish also tend to swallow the entire lure, and the treble hook is difficult to remove without injuring the fish. Consequently, it's almost impossible to release small cats unharmed. Use dip baits mainly in sluggish waters when you plan on keeping small fish.

SPONGE BAITS

These are "souped-up" dip baits. About the only difference in the two is consistency. Sponge baits are thinner, more liquid than solid, so a sponge-covered treble hook is used to soak up the bait for fishing. Catfish scent formulas are also fished in this manner.

Fishing sponge baits is simple. Dip a sponge hook in the bait, squish it with a stick till it's saturated, then cast the sponge rig out in a likely looking spot. The bait bleeds out more slowly than a typical dip bait, but quicker than a good doughbait, so check your sponge every 10 minutes or so to be sure it's well soaked with bait. Sponge baits are super clean, rate well on cat appeal and hookability, and are effective even in swift currents.

TUBE BAITS

Packaged in long, soft-plastic tubes like toothpaste, tube baits are usually fished in specially made plastic lures or protein-based bladders that come in a variety of different shapes and sizes. A narrow slit in one side permits bait to be squeezed in, and small holes let the bait melt slowly into the water. Tube baits can also be applied to sponge hooks, catfish worms or even into mouths and gills of minnows and shad.

Tube baits offer several advantages over other stinkbaits. For catters who abhor the waiting game, tube bait lures can be repeatedly cast and retrieved just like other artificials. They work well in heavy currents and hot weather where other stinkbaits often fail. Also, few other stinkbaits are versatile enough to be used in so many different ways.

The biggest drawback is cost. Tube baits are clean, there's no worry about hookability, and cat appeal is about average. But on a per-ounce basis, tube baits often cost 50 to 100 percent more than other commercial stinkbaits. On top of that, the special hook often costs as much as a 6-ounce tube of bait, escalating the cost even higher. Fishing tube baits can be great fun, but unless money is no object, save them for those occasions when nothing else works.

CHUNK BAITS

These are usually packaged in cellophane or plastic bags and containers. Each bag contains dozens of individual pieces of bait, which are solid, smelly and about the size of a grape. Many manufacturers don't package the bait in resealable bags, so carry your own to keep opened chunk baits moist and fresh.

Most chunk baits don't rate very high on cat appeal. They generally melt too slowly, if at all, so a cat must be really close to home in on your offering unless you have time to sit and wait. Chunk baits score well on cleanliness, leaving your hands stinky but not messy. But hookability falls somewhere in the mid-range. Until you get the hang of casting it, you'll probably sling off about half the chunks you stick on the hook. Chunk baits are better than dough-baits in this respect, but it would be a refreshing change

---

HOMEMADE STINKBAITS

There are hundreds of recipes for homemade stinkbaits. Here are three you can try.

CHEESY DOUGHBAIT

1 cup Limburger cheese
1 cup hamburger meat
2 tablespoons garlic powder
1/2 cup flour

Run hamburger through a food processor or blender to make a thick paste. Add cheese and garlic powder; knead thoroughly. Add enough flour to bring dough to the desired consistency.

MINNOW OR SHAD DIP BAIT

Allow a mess of mashed minnows or shad to decay in a buried plastic freezer container. (Don't use a glass container as it could explode!) A small sponge on a hook saturated with this bait works well to attract channel catfish.

TROTLINE CHUNK BAIT

1 cup yellow cornmeal
1 cup flour
1/4 teaspoon anise oil
1 tin sardines, packed in oil

Mix all ingredients in a large bowl. Add small amounts of water to form a breadlike dough. Form dough into balls the size of a Ping-Pong ball and drop into boiling water for 3 minutes. Remove, drain on paper towels and allow to cool.

---

to find a commercial chunk bait that stays hooked on every cast.

Although chunk baits leave something to be desired as rod-and-reel baits, they edge out all competitors in the stinkbait market when used on a trotline. Slow-melting bait is OK when trotlining. And chunk baits are quick and easy to hook – a plus when baiting a hundred or more hooks. A piece of chunk bait on every third hook attracts cats to other baits on a trotline.

4

CATFISHING
TECHNIQUES

Still-Fishing

S till-fishing for catfish is a sit-and-wait game. The angler presents a bait on or near the bottom, then waits for a catfish to find it. Catfish have keen senses, and there are times when moving a bait around is counterproductive because it's difficult for feeding cats to find. The juices and scent of a bait disperse through the water and are detected by the catfish's senses of smell and taste. The cat then uses those senses to zero in on the prospective dinner. If the bait is taken away too fast, however, all bets are off. That's why, in many cases, it's best to let a bait sit for a while before moving it. Still-fishing lets you do just that.

STILL-FISHING FROM A BOAT

The obvious advantage of still-fishing from a boat is mobility. Bank-bound anglers are limited in their choice of fishing areas, while boat anglers are limited only by the size of their fuel tank.

You'll need at least one and preferably two anchors for this type of catfishing. One is better than none, but with a single anchor, your boat is likely to swing in the breeze or current, tangling lines and requiring you to frequently move your rigs. Using two anchors, one on each end of the boat, keeps the boat stationary so your rigs can be spread out and cover more water.

For this method to be effective, the angler must determine areas where catfish are likely to be feeding. A cat's superb senses allow it to zero in on a bait several yards away, but a bait placed too far outside their realm of sensory ability goes undetected. Try to pinpoint prime fishing areas, then narrow your fishing zones down to a few best spots.

For example, a riprapped bank is an ideal place to find catfish. But riprap may extend for hundreds of yards, and cats won't be equally dispersed along its entire length. Look for features that concentrate catfish – a large snag

within the rocks, rocks of a different size (big boulders within a long stretch of smaller rocks) or points.

Likewise, when fishing along an inundated creek channel, look for some nuance of structural difference that may attract catfish – a pocket or point on the channel edge, a stump field or cluster of timber, a deeper hole along the outside bend. Position your boat for best access to the structure you've chosen, then cast your bait to that spot and wait for a bite.

GOOD STILL-FISHING LOCATIONS

POSITION your boat near a hump and target cover areas. Fish shallow reaches at night, deep edges during the day.

SET UP below tributaries, or at the junction of two rivers. Fish the current seam that forms just down-stream.

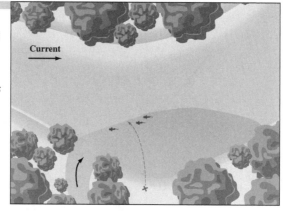

SHORE-FISH the head of a deep pool on the out-side bend of a river. The best pools have fall-en trees or snags in them.

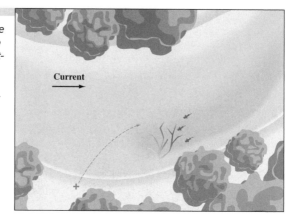

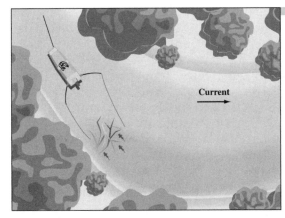

ANCHOR your boat at the top end of river pools. The best have big boulders or woody snags for current breaks.

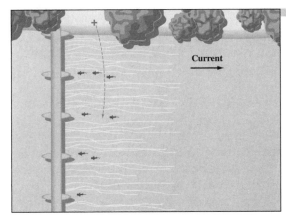

CAST your rig to grooves of slow water that form between open gates. Cats hold in these slack-water pockets.

FISH around man-made shelters common in many reservoirs. The best are close to a channel edge or drop-off.

When using multiple lines, it's best to have rod holders strategically placed around the boat to hold the rods, and the reels should be equipped with free-spool clickers. This way, the lines are spread out, and a fish can take a bait without pulling a rod in the water. When using a reel without a clicker, keep your combo in your hand, with a finger on the line to detect bites. Rods leaned against the side of the boat can get yanked into the drink by even small catfish. If half an hour passes without a bite, move to another location and set up again. Likewise, if catfish are biting and the action suddenly stops, it's best to move.

STILL-FISHING FROM SHORE

Most catfisherman, up to 70 percent in some areas, fish from shore. Some do so simply because it's convenient, while others do it out of necessity. For most catters, though, fishing from shore is simply "the way it's done." You and a buddy build a fire on the riverbank, bait up a few rigs, and prop your rods on forked sticks. A cat will bite sooner or later, and the action starts. But if not, it's an enjoyable outing anyway.

If the action part of the outing is as important as the aesthetics, be sure to pick a bankfishing site within casting distance of prime catfishing areas. This might be a clearing on shore near the outside bend of a river or a gravel bar adjacent a deep hole on a small stream. The best areas have flat, brush-free banks where casting is easy.

Ideally, you should be able to walk from one good fishing site to another without any problems. If catching fish is your top priority, don't sit in one spot hour after hour if nothing's happening. Fish for 15 to 30 minutes, and if nothing is biting, move to the next spot. It's typical to find a good hole and catch several cats, then the action tapers off. This is why frequent moves can increase your catch rate.

Of course, leapfrogging isn't to everyone's liking. And in some areas, it's impossible due to the lack of good bankfishing sites. If this is the case, cast your bait to the best-looking spot you can reach, then prepare to wait out your quarry. Place your rod in a rod holder, put the reel in free-spool, flip on the bait clicker, and relax until the action starts. This method may not put lots of catfish on your stringer, but it's a great way to target trophy fish.

IN MANY STATES, it's legal to pre-bait or "chum" a selected fishing area in order to attract and concentrate catfish. Check your state's regulations to be sure. If it's OK, give chumming a try.

Set the Table

Chumming works best on waters with little or no current. You want the chum to settle around the area you are fishing, not wash downstream.

Many manufacturers sell pre-packaged chum over the counter, but if you're ambitious, you can make your own.

To begin, pour a gallon of wheat and/or milo into a container and cover with water. Place in a sunny location outdoors, uncovered, and allow to sit several days until the mixture sours. The worse the mixture smells, the better catfish like it.

When you reach your fishing area, scatter a half-gallon of chum around the area you intend to fish. Sling it like you would when feeding chickens. You want catfish to pick up the feed kernel by kernel, so they don't get full. Lower a regular bait (baitfish, nightcrawler, etc.) on the bottom with the grain, and with luck, a catfish will come along and suck it up. If cats are actively foraging, they'll quickly move into the area.

Tailwater areas below dams rank among the best for shore-fishing enthusiasts. The U.S. Army Corps of Engineers, the Tennessee Valley Authority and other agencies provide river-side walkways, fishing piers and other shoreline facilities to accommodate visiting anglers. Blue, flathead and channel catfish concentrate in huge numbers in dam tailwaters, especially during their upstream runs in spring. Because of this, your odds of catching a trophy cat are above average.

Tailwater anglers usually fish with 10- to 14-foot fiberglass rods and sinkers that weigh up to 8 ounces, which allow for the long casts necessary to reach prime catfish areas from shore, and get to the bottom fast in the strong current. Bottom rigs of any sort work, but most anglers opt for a three-way rig, or a slip-sinker rig with either a bell or egg sinker.

One of the best places to consistently catch catfish below a dam is the slack-water areas between open gates known as grooves (p. 61). To fish these, cast your rig into a groove and leave it there for about 15 minutes. If there are no takers, lift your rod tip high to pick the weight up, and let the current wash it downstream a few feet. Then let the weight down again, and repeat the process. By doing this, an angler can cover a long stretch of bottom from a single spot on shore.

When there's good water flow through or over a dam, the roiling waters directly below generally provide the best catfishing, but don't overlook other prime tailwater areas. These include scour holes at the end of wing dams, the downstream side of underwater boulders, retaining walls, riprap, spillways and lock-wall edges.

Although tailraces are the most popular spots to fish cats from shore, there are others that can provide good catfishing as well. Fishing piers are becoming more numerous across the country, and are often built on prime catfishing waters. The best part about piers is they offer fishing opportunities for everyone. Most are wheelchair accessible, and provide safe, convenient locations to take the whole family catfishing. Look for buoys around piers that mark sunken fish structures, such as old Christmas trees and brush piles. These often hold numbers of catfish.

The confluence of two rivers is another good spot to try for catfish. Keep your rig near current-breaking structure such as the current seams and sand or gravel bars that form when two rivers meet.

No matter where you fish from shore, be sure you have the right equipment. Never use tackle that is too light; remember, cats generally aren't line shy, so use as heavy a line as your equipment can handle. The chance of hooking a trophy fish is always there, and a big cat can be tougher to land from shore than from a boat. A net is best for landing large fish, but if you're fishing alone, beaching the fish may be necessary. And finally, bring lots of terminal tackle – you're going to lose a lot of it to snags – that's just a fact of shorefishing.

STILL-FISHING TIPS

•*Carry* two anchors to position a boat sideways in a good hole. This way rods are spread out to cover more water and avoid tangles.

•*Use* a clip-on float to detect bites. With the rod in a holder, pull line down and attach float so it falls off when reeling. When a cat bites, the float rises.

•*Tie* light line between the sinker and swivel of a three-way rig. Then, if you get snagged, the sinker breaks off and you salvage the hook and swivel.

Safe Handling of Catfish

YOUR SMILE OF SUCCESS will turn to a grimace of pain if you handle catfish improperly. Although their teeth are small and sandpaperlike, big cats can bite with enough force to crush a finger. And all cats have sharp pectoral and dorsal fin spines that can inflict nasty wounds on careless anglers. Follow these tips to avoid unfortunate encounters.

•To hold small catfish or bullheads, approach the fish from tail to head on the belly side. Move your hands up to the base of the pectoral and dorsal fins and squeeze the fish firmly so it is unable to move. A fishing towel can help you maintain a good grip on slippery fish.

•If you plan to release a cat, don't handle it at all. Keep it in the water and remove the hook with pliers, or cut the line.

•Don't put your fingers in a catfish's mouth, especially if it's a big blue or channel cat. Even gloved fingers can get smashed in a big cat's maw.

•Always use great care when swinging a catfish into the boat or on shore. This is when many anglers are wounded by the sharp spines.

•Land big cats with a landing net or gaff. If you plan to keep your catch, thump it hard between the eyes with a fishing club or hammer. Then handle it by the gills with gloved hands. Bare hands can be cut by the bony gill arches inside the gill cover.

•Never toss a cat when releasing it or giving it to a fishing partner. The barbed spines can slice the thrower's fingers, and the person on the receiving end could find a spine embedded in a leg, arm or hand.

•Always pay attention and use extreme care when handling any catfish. Treat all wounds for infection. See a doctor immediately for serious wounds or those that get infected.

Drift-Fishing

Drift-fishing doesn't fit the traditional "sit-and-wait" approach used by most catfish anglers. But think about this. If you anchor a bait on bottom with a sinker, you must rely on the catfish's acute senses to find the bait. Drift-fishing, however, helps you help the cats find the bait. It's an active approach that often means more catfish on waters where it can be used.

Two basic methods of drift-fishing are commonly employed in catfishing – drift-fishing in a boat, and drift-fishing baits beneath a bobber.

DRIFT-FISHING IN A BOAT

This is a commonly used catfishing technique in late winter and early spring. As winter passes and water warms, catfish leave cold-weather haunts and scatter, making them difficult to pinpoint. The same thing occurs any time water in a lake or river is quickly rising or falling. Drift-fishing allows the angler to cover more water and find these widely scattered fish.

Drift-fishing doesn't need to be complicated. Fish from the same boat you already use when catfishing. Use the same rods, reels, line and other tackle already in service. Use one rod or a dozen, but determine beforehand if there are any restrictions. In some areas, you can fish with as many poles as you dare to; in others, the number is limited.

If the wind's blowing, you can get by without a trolling motor, but unless you're on an exceptionally large body of water where you can make an extremely long drift, you're not likely to catch as many catfish. Wind drifting is typically a one-way, time-consuming affair – make a drift, take up the

POPULAR RIGS FOR DRIFT-FISHING

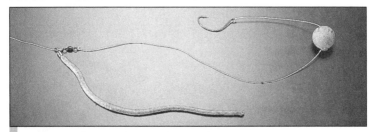

Float rig with a snagless "slinky" weight

Keel-weighted trolling-sinker rig

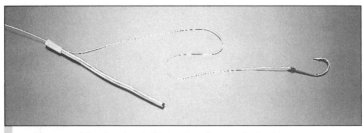

In-line pencil lead sinker held in place by surgical tubing

rods, motor back up, reset the rods, drift again. An electric trolling motor, on the other hand, allows constant fishing without fuss. It also permits you to vary your speed and control direction, important factors when trying to get fussy catfish to bite. A small outboard serves the purpose for some anglers, but most prefer the quiet hum of an electric motor over the noisy drone of a gas engine. Catfish seem to as well.

If you'll be using several rods, and most drift-fishermen do, you'll want some way to hold them at the ready. A few sturdy clamp-on rod holders fitted around the transom work OK in some situations. But it's better to use permanently mounted models that won't be torn off the first time a big cat hits. These are available in many different styles. Purchase those that work best on your boat, then place them at strategic positions in a semicircle around the forward or rear half of the craft.

When rods are in place, a drift-fishing boat looks like a big spider moving across the water with legs pointing in all directions. Start by using a variety of baits rigged at different depths. For instance, if you're using six poles, rig two with pieces of cut-bait, two with chunk-type stinkbaits and the other two with minnows. Set two baits so they drift just above the bottom, two at mid-depths, and two just a few feet beneath the surface. This lets you test different baits and depths until you find the catfish's preference that particular day. Once it's established that catfish are favoring a certain depth or bait, then rig and set the rest of the rods accordingly.

A float rig (opposite page, top) is ideal for fishing near the bottom while drifting. The main line is run through the eye of a pencil weight, a type of bottom-bouncer sinker constructed from a long plastic or nylon tube filled with lead. A ball-bearing swivel is tied below the weight to keep it from sliding down. A 24- to 36-inch leader is then tied to the lower eye of the swivel. A small bobber or float is affixed in the middle of the leader, and a wide gap hook is tied at the end. The float suspends the baited hook above bottom to help prevent snags.

For mid-depth and near-surface presentations, use a trolling-sinker rig (opposite page, middle). These sinkers are overlooked by many catfishermen, but they are extremely useful when drifting for catfish. Keeled or torpedo-shaped models track well with little side-to-side action. Planing versions have wings that cause the sinker to dive and achieve more depth. Bead-chain swivels are molded into most to prevent line twist. To rig, simply tie your main line to the front eye of the sinker, then attach your hook to the rear eye with a 2- to 3-foot leader. Vary the sinker size according to water depth and drifting speed.

Another virtually snagless rig that is effective for drift-fishing is one that incorporates a pencil lead sinker (p. 130, bottom). Simply slide a small piece of surgical tubing on your line, then tie on a hook. Cut a length of pencil lead and insert one end into the tubing and slide the sinker up the line to the desired distance. If the sinker is too heavy, just snip a section of lead off to make it lighter.

Speed is considered by many to be the most important aspect of drift-fishing, but there's no magic formula to determine what speed is best under a given set of conditions. On some days you may have to inch your boat along to get strikes. On other days you'll have to troll so fast you'll wonder how catfish could possibly catch your bait. When you find the productive speed, try to maintain it, even when wind and current push your boat ahead or drive it back.

Savvy anglers experiment with different drift speeds until they determine what is most effective. In muddy or heavily stained water, you might have to drift-fish very slowly for catfish to find your bait. In a clear-water lake, fast-moving baits may be very effective. The key word here is "experiment." Try to figure how catfish are likely to react in the type of water you're fishing, then adapt your tactics to conform with those expectations. But if your game plan doesn't produce within a short time, try something different.

Once you determine the speed catfish seem to favor, do your best to maintain that speed without variation until you no longer catch fish. One mistake anglers often make is drifting at the same motor thrust traveling against the wind as when headed with the wind. On an otherwise still lake, you travel faster with the wind than against it, assuming you never reposition your electric-motor throttle. Therefore, in order to maintain your ideal trolling speed, you must adjust the throttle up or down depending on

GOOD LOCATIONS TO DRIFT-FISH WITH A BOAT

A LARGE FLAT adjacent to a creek channel that is sparsely covered with snags holds fish almost year-round, and is easier to drift than an irregular bottom.

RIPRAP SHORELINES and other gradual breaks often hold pockets of catfish. Drift-fishing these areas lets you find fish quicker than still-fishing.

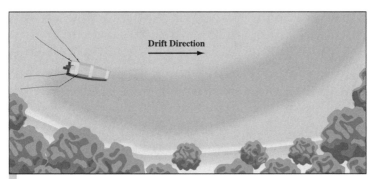

OXBOWS usually vary little in depth, and catfish are sometimes scattered. Drift-fishing near the deepest water is the best way to locate and catch these fish.

which way you are traveling. On extremely windy days, you may even have to run the trolling motor in reverse to keep from drifting too fast.

The same is true when in current. When traveling against the flow, you must increase the throttle to maintain the same speed you had when traveling downstream. Fail to do so, and your speed changes drastically. So will the number of catfish you'll catch.

These factors may explain why, on a particular day, you'll catch catfish when drifting in one direction and not in the other.

Some anglers start their drift blind. In other words, they have no idea what type of structure or cover is below. They simply start drifting and hope their hit-and-miss tactics produce more hits than misses.

If you want to cut down on your looking time and add to your hooking time, buy a good flasher or liquid crystal graph. Catfish may be roaming, but they'll still be near structure or along the thermocline. By first looking at a contour map and a quick check of prominent bottom changes with sonar, you could be catching catfish instead of wandering aimlessly.

DRIFT-FISHING WITH BOBBERS

You don't always need a boat to drift-fish. When wading or bankfishing on a river, you can drift your bait beneath a bobber. This allows the bait to move naturally downstream, responding to current, flowing through rapids and settling enticingly in holes. Bobber rigs also provide the best way to thoroughly work eddies of swirling water behind fallen trees, boulders and other current breaks.

Many bobbers are clipped or pegged in place on the line, but this type of rigging is cumbersome to cast. A slip-bobber rig works best because the bobber slides freely on the line, allowing you to reel all your terminal tackle close to the rod tip for easier casting. The bobber style is determined by current and bait size. In heavy current, or when medium to large baits are used, use a larger, rounder, more buoyant bobber. In low to moderate flow, or when using small baits, a smaller cigar-shaped bobber is fine.

Position the bobber stop so your bait hangs a foot or two above, not on, the stream bottom. Add just enough weight to hold the bait down and stand the bobber up, then let the rig drift naturally in the current, guiding it alongside catfish holding structure. With a little practice and a long rod to keep your line up off the water surface, you can become quite adept at steering the rig past holding areas with little worry about hangups.

Keep a tight line at all times. A slack line bows downstream ahead of the bait. This leaves you in a bad position for setting the hook when a catfish hits. All the energy of the hook set is used taking in the slack.

Feed line as the bait moves downstream. If the rig hangs up, your bobber will tip over or stop. Lift it a bit to get the bait moving again. Then tease the rig around boulders, ease it alongside fallen trees and work it through holes below rapids. Drift by one side of a hole, then down the other and finally right down the middle. If nothing happens after you've worked an area thoroughly, move your bobber stop up the line and drift through deeper. Or move downstream to another spot and try again. If possible, shift sides of the river every now and then to present baits in every likely spot as you move.

Trotlining

Trotlining is an age-old method of catching fish. Some say it doesn't qualify as true angling at all. Others call it "lazy man's fishing." A few go so far as to declare it unsporting.

Trotlining is, however, a traditional method of catfishing. It is legal in many states and regularly practiced on numerous prime catfishing waters throughout the United States. Done properly, by conservation-minded anglers, it seldom hurts a catfish population. In fact, many southern fisheries biologists maintain trotlining is an important technique for preventing overpopulation in certain bodies of water.

A trotline is simply a stout line placed horizontally across an expanse of water. Tied at regular intervals along the main line are short lines with baited hooks. For some now-forgotten reason, these short lines were once called trots, hence the name trotline. The term "troutline," which is often heard, is incorrect.

Trotlining is the most productive hook-and-line method for catching large quantities of catfish. This stands to reason as a single trotline can have as many as 1,000 hooks. Many commercial fishermen rely on trotlines for their catch of catfish, and in some areas, the number of hooks is unrestricted so long as the fisherman is properly licensed. When trotlines are used by sport fishermen, however, there is usually a restriction on the number of hooks and lines allowed. Check local regulations before setting lines. In some states, trotlining is illegal. In most, it is limited by a variety of restrictions.

Ready-made trotlines are available at many tackle distributors, but beware of cheap products with poor-quality components that could break under the strain of a heavy fish. Most trotliners custom-make all their lines to work under the variety of conditions encountered on the water.

TIE an overhand knot in the main line, leaving a 6-inch dropper loop. Space the loops at 5-foot intervals.

ATTACH a big barrel swivel to the dropper by threading it through the eye and back around the swivel.

CUT a 12-inch section of a separate, smaller diameter cord, double it, and tie an overhand knot with the tag ends.

PUSH the smaller cord through the other eye of the swivel, and loop it back through itself.

ADD a hook by pushing the looped end of the smaller cord through the hook eye, then loop around the hook.

FINISHED trots should be 12 to 18 inches long and tied every 5 feet.

The main line of the trotline is made of heavy-duty nylon cord. Some catfishermen use 200- to 300-pound test, but heavier is better because the large diameter is easier on the hands when pulling yourself along to run and bait the line. At least 600-pound test is recommended. The length of the main line varies depending on the size of the water and the number of hooks used. Most trotlines, however, are 25 to 125 yards long with 20 to 100 hooks.

DIFFERENT WAYS TO SET A TROTLINE

SHORELINE TO A SNAG. Use a piece of rebar stake to secure the line to shore if no tie-off point is present. With a weight in the middle, hooks hang at different depths.

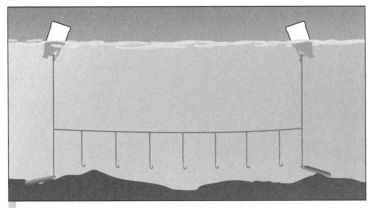

WEIGHT TO WEIGHT. In snag-free waters and off-shore areas, a line like this works best. Use heavy weights at each end to keep big cats from taking the line.

Trots or "stagings" – the short lines to which the hooks are attached – are made of 100- to 200-pound-test nylon and are 1 to 2 feet long. To prevent catfish from twisting off the hooks, the trots hang from big swivels on the main line. The swivels are slipped on the main line at 2- to 3-foot intervals and held in place with crimp-on metal brads (available from many catfishing outfitters) attached to the main line on both sides of each swivel.

SHORELINE TO A WEIGHT. Use a burlap bag full of rocks to weight the end of the line. This type line is best when fishing perpendicular to shore in heavy current.

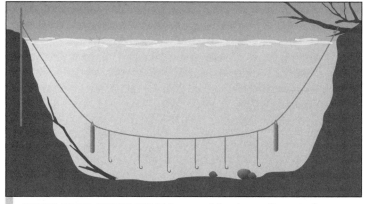

SHORELINE TO SHORELINE. This type of line is excellent at tributary mouths and narrow coves. Try to place the line near good structure and cover.

Thirty-six inches of line makes an 18-inch trot. Pass the line's two loose ends together through the bottom eye of the swivel, then tie a knot to hold the trot in place, leaving a hanging loop of line approximately 18 inches long. Attach the hook by passing the loop through the hook's eye then over the hook point. Cinch the loop snug against the hook's eye, and you're ready to rig another. A better way is to attach each swivel directly to the main line (p. 137).

Because the trots are made of heavy line, you'll have to use hooks with large eyes. Limerick and circle hooks with a tinned finish are popular styles, in sizes 2/0 to 6/0, depending on the bait being used. Use larger hooks to target trophy fish with large baits.

In most situations, 5-pound weights are placed along the line at intervals of about 50 feet to hold the line near the bottom. These can be rocks, concrete blocks, window weights or pieces of scrap metal.

There are times, however, when a suspended line works best. Blue cats, for instance, are often caught on lines set several feet off the bottom, especially in fast-rising water. In such a case, use smaller weights to hold the line down to the desired level. Always keep the line far enough below the surface so it won't tangle in the propeller of a passing boat. Use floating trotlines only if you plan to sit and watch them constantly, or in private waters with minimal boat traffic.

The ends of the line can be secured in several ways. One is to stretch the line between two snags or between a shoreline tree and a snag out in the water. Another is to tie one end to a tree or snag, then anchor the other end with a heavy weight. In this case, you can tie a jug to a line and fasten it to the weight to mark its location. If no trees or snags are available for tie-off points, use weights on both ends of the line, each marked with a jug. Mark long lines along their entire length with regularly spaced jugs.

You can set a trotline anywhere and catch a few cats, but to improve your success, take time to pinpoint a prime location. Look for the same areas you'd target when fishing with rod and reel – for instance, holes, outside bends, tributary mouths and channel edges in rivers; riprapped banks, shallow wooded flats, creek channels and tributaries in lakes and reservoirs.

Once you've zeroed in on a spot, determine how to lay the line. Sometimes it's best to run it perpendicular to shore first, with one end in shallow water and the other end out deep. This way you can determine the depth at which cats are feeding. Once this is known, move the line to a position parallel to shore in water of that depth.

You're using numerous hooks, so bring plenty of bait. What you use depends on what type catfish you want to catch. If small cats are the target, use a chunk-style stinkbait, chicken liver or crawfish. For big channels and blues, cut-bait is best. For big flatheads and other trophy-class cats, large, frisky live bait outperforms all else. Regional favorites include goldfish, shiners, small carp, bullheads, sunfish and large suckers.

Most trotliners set lines during the day, then bait them right at dark. (If lines are baited when the sun is up, gar, turtles and other pests strip the hooks.) The lines are then run periodically throughout the night and again right at dawn. Lines should always be removed when you leave, so there's no chance of another angler or animal getting tangled in the hooks.

Use special care when running the lines, too. Most trotliners work in pairs, for camaraderie and division of labor. Each person should keep a sharp knife handy, either on their belt or strapped to a leg, to cut the line if someone is accidentally hooked. More than one trotliner has drowned after getting snagged by a hook and pulled under by a trotline weight.

TROTLINING TIPS

• *Set* trotlines with a partner. One person controls the boat while the other baits or checks the line. This is by far the easiest and safest way to fish.

• *Strap* a knife to your leg or belt when trotlining. Should you get hooked, you can cut the line before getting pulled in.

• *Store* your trotlines in a garbage pail when not in use. This way, the hooks won't tangle, and the line goes out smoothly when resetting.

ONE OF MY MOST SPECIAL culinary memories began on a rustic houseboat on southeast Arkansas' White River. A friend invited me to stay on his houseboat while on a photo shoot, and while there, Ralph Griffin invited us upstream to share a meal on his boat. Ralph, a resident of Jonesboro, Arkansas, served as a commissioner for the Arkansas Game & Fish Commission from 1969 through 1976. He's an expert catfisherman, and true to form, he caught several big cats the morning we arrived. One fish served as the entrée for a simple yet unforgettable meal. Ralph prepared catfish fillets fried golden brown, mouthwatering hushpuppies and fresh vegetables from his garden. His recipe for fried catfish – Ralph's Three Rivers Catfish – is still my favorite.

Ralph Griffin, Cat Man
by Keith Sutton

Claud (left) and Ralph with a 30-pound flathead.

I knew immediately Ralph was serious about catching big cats. The livewell on his houseboat is a perforated metal tank the size of a pick-up cab resting through the boat floor into the river below. It's lifted from the water with a big winch, and when Ralph cranked it up that first day, there were three dandy cats inside – a 35-pound blue, a 20-pound flathead and a 15-pound blue – all from a single morning's run.

Ralph's houseboat is home base during his frequent visits to Three Rivers Country – the region where the White, Arkansas and Mississippi rivers converge. This area offers action-packed fishing for giant cats equal to that found anywhere on the continent, with millions of pounds of channel, blue and flathead catfish caught yearly. Thirty-pound cats hardly raise an eyebrow, and cats weighing 50 pounds and more are caught here with astounding regularity.

Trotlining is the most popular catfishing method in Three Rivers Country, and this is the technique used most often by Ralph Griffin. He sets most of his lines on the Mississippi River near the river's confluence with the White. To increase the chance of success, he often uses six or more lines, all placed in known catfish hideouts.

I accompanied him the day we met to run his lines. They were all stretched from willows and other shoreline anchor points out into the river, perpendicular to the current. The end of each was attached to a heavy weight to keep the current from swinging it in to the bank, and because the trotlines stretched from shallow water into deep, they covered a variety of water levels. "With the lines set that way," Ralph said, "at least some of the hooks are going to be at the level catfish are feeding. If cats are feeding shallow, most of my catch will be on the shallow end of the lines. If more cats are feeding deep, the opposite is true." The fish we caught this morning were all on the shallow end of the lines.

Ralph baits his lines with live fish. Goldfish are preferred because they remain lively on the hook for extended periods, but shiners are used in a pinch and also produce well. His hooks run 5/0, 6/0 and bigger to hold the monstrous cats he sometimes catches.

These tactics work. Each year Ralph catches 10 to 15 cats over 30 pounds. His largest to date is a 57-pound flathead, and he's also taken blues up to 47.

His expertise as a fisherman, however, pales in comparison to his culinary skills. If you don't believe it, try Ralph's Three Rivers Catfish (p. 187). As they say, the proof is in the pudding, or catfish, as the case may be.

Jug Fishing

"Thar she blows!"

When a big catfish pulls a jug under, the call rings out. Of course, the cat isn't as big as Moby Dick, but this is as close to whale hunting as you can get in a lake or river.

For pure fun, nothing equals jug fishing for cats. Save a few empty milk or soda jugs, tie some line on them, add some hooks, bait 'em up and you're ready for action. The only other things you need are a boat and paddle (or trolling motor) for pursuit and a big landing net to corral your quarry.

Any jugs work, but use only those previously filled with non-toxic substances. One- to 2-liter soda bottles are ideal. They won't race away too fast if it's windy, they're big enough to be easily seen, and the typical catfish can't hold one under for long. Paint them so they're more visible on the water. Fluorescent orange, chartreuse and black work well, but avoid white and light colors that blend with the reflective surface of the water.

For convenience's sake, rig jugs at home. Any heavy line works; cats aren't line shy. But soft line – Dacron or nylon – won't get as coiled and hard-to-handle as monofilament. Use something stout – 50-pound test or more – just in case you have to snatch a line and battle a big cat to the boat. You can tie directly to the jug's handle or neck if you like, but your jugs will tip better, signaling strikes, if you attach line to the cap instead. To do this, simply drill a small hole through the cap, run the line through from outside, and tie it to a washer so it won't pull back through. Screw the cap back on and you're set.

Line length is determined by a combination of water, wind and bottom conditions. Tie plenty on your jug, then lengthen or shorten it as needed. You can do this by

wrapping line around the jug and securing it with tape or a rubber band, or by loosening the washer and stuffing line inside the jug. The latter method is best if you want the jugs to tip up when a cat takes the bait.

If you don't mind the extra expense, you can make rigging even simpler by attaching a yo-yo (Auto-Fisher) to the cap of each jug. Then simply pull out the amount of line needed, set the catch to hold the line in place, and start fishing. The spring-wound trip mechanism in the yo-yo also provides an extra measure of hook set. This is very helpful since jugs offer only slight resistance as compared to a trotline or setting a hook with rod and reel.

For cats up to 15 pounds, use one or two 1/0 to 3/0 hooks. If two hooks are used, rig one above the other, to test different depths. When targeting heavyweight cats with large baits, use bigger hooks – from 6/0 to 10/0. Be sure each hook is needle sharp.

You can also tie a bell sinker above or below each hook to hold the bait near bottom or to slow movement of the jugs when it's windy. Add your favorite bait – cut-bait, nightcrawlers, catalpa worms, chunk bait, etc. – then release the jugs several feet apart and let them drift in the breeze or current.

It's important to float your rigs near catfish-attracting structure and cover, but try to fish a few feet away from snags so your jugs won't hang up. If they do, you'll be continually stopping, and the rest of your flotilla may scatter and drift from sight. Follow at a distance so you don't spook fish, but be ready to react the moment you see action.

Each jug acts like a giant bobber. When a cat starts nibbling, the jug stops and bobbles. When a cat swallows the bait, the jug takes on a life of its own, zipping across the water at a high rate of speed or disappearing beneath the surface. This is where you holler, "Thar she blows!" And the fun begins.

To land a catfish on a jug line, approach the jug as quickly as possible, then either grab the jug or sweep a landing net under it to catch the line. A pole with a hook on the end also works well. (Never grab the jug line with your hands; you could get tangled or cut.) If a small cat has taken the bait, retrieving the jug is easy. But if a big cat is on, the chase begins. The jug may sound, then pop up several yards away, time and time again before you get close enough to snatch the rig. Wary catfish often zip away every time you get near. That's why two anglers are better than one in this sport. One controls the boat during pursuit, while the other stands ready to capture the fleeing cat. Both should wear life jackets, in case of an unexpected spill.

Jug fishing is not allowed in several states, while a few others regulate the number of jugs each angler can use. It's difficult to keep up with more than a dozen anyway, so limit the number you use, and be sure none are lost and left to litter the lake or river.

HOW TO RUN JUG LINES

•*Toss* jug lines downstream or downwind of your boat. Keep jugs fairly close together so you can watch them.

•*Watch* for any jugs that bob erratically or go under. Pursue the jug once it starts swimming away.

•*Grab* the jug, not the line. If it is a big fish, you can cut your hands on the line as the fish struggles.

TIPS FOR JUG FISHING

•*Drill* a hole in the middle of a plastic bottle cap, and tie the line to a washer. Screw the cap back on.

•*Paint* jugs a bright color so they are easier to see on the water.

•*Tape* the hook to the side of a jug when not in use. This helps avoid tangles.

Limblining

n its simplest form, a limbline is nothing more than a baited hook and line tied to a stout yet springy limb overhanging the water. When a catfish bites, the limb's flexibility keeps the fish from breaking the line. These setups are also known as bush hooks or brush lines.

The line for limblines should be at least 25-pound test, preferrably braided Dacron. A 2/0 to 4/0 steel hook with a large eye is recommended by most experts. A weight should be added just above the hook when using a large baitfish, or if there is a strong current. Limblining works best at night, so use a piece of cloth or reflective tape to mark each set so it can be easily found with a flashlight.

Willow limbs are the best tie-offs for limblines because they're long, flexible and easy to find. But green branches of any sort work, as long as they are strong and pliable, and provide a good tie-off point above the water.

If pliable limbs are unavailable, alternative methods can be used. Traditionalists sometimes use solid, inflexible limbs and tie a section of rubber inner tube into the line to provide the flex. More sophisticated limbliners use yo-yos, mechanical, spring-loaded devices that have a trigger mechanism that helps set the hook and allows a fish to run a short distance.

Bobby poles are cut saplings, usually willows, that are pushed into the bank and used as tie-off points. They are placed in areas where overhanging limbs are absent, such as riprapped banks. Cut them long enough to reach well out over the water when stabbed into the bank at an angle.

A variety of baits and presentations are used by limbliners, depending on the size fish they are after. Some use cut-bait or crawfish rigged so the bait lies directly on the bottom. Others prefer commercial stinkbaits, night crawlers or catalpa worms presented 2 or 3 feet beneath the surface. Most, however, prefer lively fish, frogs or salamanders rigged on short lines so the bait wiggles and thrashes right at the water's surface. Tie to your anchor point, then cut off enough line to keep the baited hook just below the surface. This is a deadly setup for attracting hungry catfish.

Small bluegills, goldfish and leopard frogs work great on limblines. These hardy baits swim for hours on end without tiring. When targeting a heavyweight cat, try a 6- to 8-inch carp, sucker or bullhead, or even a hand-size sunfish. Bigger baits make more commotion and attract bigger cats.

To begin limblining, pinpoint areas where branches overhang good catfish habitat. The best spots are deep outside

TIPS FOR LIMBLINING

CUT a 1-inch section from an old tire inner tube and tie it in your line if no flexible limbs are available.

USE a circle hook on a limbline. This style hooks catfish in the corner of their mouth as they swim away.

RIG a weight on a limbline when using a large bait, or when fishing in heavy current.

river bends, deep pools near the mouths of tributaries, holes below riffles or sandbars, and any other place where current collects food.

Most expert limbliners agree conditions are best in spring when ravenous catfish are more likely to be roaming the shallows. Green timber flooded during spring overflows holds substantial numbers of catfish, especially channel cats.

When fishing in spring or early summer just prior to the spawn, cats frequent steep banks more than shallow, gradually sloping ones. Rocky banks and those with undercuts and log piles are particularly productive. After the spawn, zero in on areas between deep-water resting areas and shallow feeding zones.

Read your state fishing regulations guide. Limblining laws vary considerably from state to state. Limbliners should also follow strict precautions regarding their sets. Never leave a limbline unattended where another angler could get hooked in it. And be certain to remove all lines at the end of a night's fishing. An abandoned line can be dangerous to wildlife and to other fishermen passing by.

Run your lines often, and get ready for fun. When you shine your light down the riverbank and see that willow branch dancing from a hundred yards, you know there's a fish waiting for you. Could be a nice eatin'-size channel cat. Then again, it could be a monster flathead or blue. You never know what's likely to turn up, but that bouncing tree limb is a sure sign of success.

TYPES OF LIMBLINES

•*Willow branches* make the best limblines because they are strong yet flexible, and are most often found hanging over water.

•*Bobby poles* are used in areas where no trees are available. Make them by cutting a long branch from a tree and sticking it into the bank.

•*Yo-Yo's* are spring-loaded devices that can be tied to any solid branch overhanging water. When a fish bites, the spring releases and sets the hook.

151

Noodling

It's the purest, most ancient form of catting. No equipment is used. No hooks, lines, poles or reels. No tackle of any sort . . . unless you consider your hands tackle.

Some call it foolish. Others prefer

idiotic. None would deny, however, those who catch catfish bare-handed are a breed unto themselves.

A variety of terms describe the practice of hand-grabbing catfish. "Noodling" is perhaps most universal, not surprising when you consider the term is derived from the word *noodle*, meaning a very stupid or silly person; a fool. "Hogging" is also used (slang for going to the limit) as are the synonyms "tickling," "grabbling" and "graveling." Call it what you will; catching giant catfish with bare hands provides an adrenaline rush not afforded by any other method of catting.

To noodle, one simply must be brave enough, or foolish enough, depending on your point of view, to reach into an underwater hole and extract the occupant. At times, this is quite simple. The occupant simply chomps down on your hand before you can react. If the creature is a catfish, your friends will pat you on the back and tell any who listen how you bravely fought the monstrous beast. If it is, instead, a snapping turtle, snake or muskrat, they'll ask how you could be so stupid as to stick your hand in a hole where you couldn't see, then give you a nickname like Nubbins, Two-Fingered Jack, or Stubby.

The best holes to noodle catfish in are old muskrat or beaver bank dens, crevices beneath rocks, hollow logs and undercut banks. Cats occupy such nooks at various times throughout the year but are most often holed up during spawning season in late spring and early summer.

Some noodlers stretch out belly-down on the bank and reach into holes. Most, however, enter shallow water – never as deep as the noodler is tall – and probe likely catfish hideouts. A short cane pole can be inserted to determine if anyone is home. If a catfish is, and it's spawning season, the fish attacks the pole, rattling it. The noodler then surfaces for air, and prepares to capture the cat.

Sometimes the hole is partially blocked with rocks, small sandbags or the noodler's body (this latter method is not recommended) to prevent the catfish's escape. If it's spawning season, however, this is unnecessary. Cats guarding a nest seldom abandon it. When a hand is inserted in the hole, the fish may nip, bite or, if large enough, actually engulf the noodler's hand. Once the cat has grabbed on, it may spin, causing the sandpaperlike teeth to scrape and shred the noodler's skin. For this reason, some noodlers wear gloves, though most believe this hinders the sense of touch necessary for determining the type of creature in the hole, its position and the best method for gaining a handhold.

When a cat attacks, the noodler attempts to grasp it by the mouth, gill cover or anything affording a grip. When noodling outside the spawning season, the hole is blocked, and the noodler tries to coax the cat's mouth open to gain a handhold. Wiggling one's fingers may do the trick, but usually, the noodler must rely on feel to find the cat's mouth or gill cover and work his fingers in. Once a noodler has a good grip, it's time to get to the surface with fish in tow. At this point, the reason for working in shallow water becomes crystal clear. If the noodler cannot quickly stand with mouth and nostrils above the water, he might find himself in a sticky predicament. Even then, battling a 50-pound-plus cat to the surface – and this is often done – may require extraordinary effort. Several square feet of the noodler's hide may be removed in the process. This is not for the faint of heart.

Scuba gear is used by some modern practitioners, many of whom place specially constructed boxes at secret spots in rivers or lakes to create their own catfish dens. A hole in one end of the box permits the diver to reach in and capture catfish inside.

Others employ hooks attached to heavy line, hooking the holed-up cat by hand, then swimming to the surface with the line where the battle continues. A pole with a breakaway hook on the end enables the catter to "noodle" without ever reaching in a hole.

None of these are pure noodling, of course, but in areas where legal, all have their proponents.

Snagging Catfish

SNAGGING is a tough way to catch catfish. To do it, the angler yanks a weighted, unbaited treble hook through the water, trying to hook a fish he cannot see. Many anglers think this is unsporting, but snagging, or snatching as it is sometimes called, is legal in many southern states and appears to be growing in popularity.

Most snagging is done during spring in dam tailwaters where catfish congregate during upstream movements. It is best during periods of power generation or when several gates are open.

Typical equipment consists of a 10- to 16-foot, heavy-action saltwater rod and a large-capacity, bait-casting or spinning reel spooled with 50- to 130-pound-test line. Two 4/0 to 9/0, needle-sharp treble hooks are tied tandem on the line, and a heavy weight (up to 20 ounces) is used to sink the hooks in swift tailwaters. (Sometimes the weight is built on the hook, which is specifically known as a snagging hook.) Once on bottom, the rig is jerked through the water until it hits a snag or a fish. Lots of terminal tackle is lost to logs and rocks.

Done conventionally, snagging is a backbreaking sport. Hundreds of casts may be made before a hook connects with a catfish, and there are times when the method is totally unproductive.

Check local regulations before noodling. In some states, it's illegal. In others, noodling is permitted but only during special seasons with a variety of restrictions. Regardless of regulations, noodlers should voluntarily restrict their harvest, protecting a resource that is extremely vulnerable to this method of fishing, especially during the spawn.

One should also consider the many dangers inherent in this unusual sport. Encountering snakes, turtles and other dangerous underwater denizens doesn't happen often, but it does happen. Crippling injuries can result. Reaching in holes can lead to serious cuts, so up-to-date tetanus shots are a must. If an arm or hand gets stuck, or if an exceptionally large cat is tackled, the noodler can drown. Risks are high, and participants should be aware that death or serious injury can result from carelessness.

But when the efforts pay off and a fish is finally on, there's plenty of exciting, white-knuckle action for the fortunate angler. If a big catfish is hooked in the tail, as often happens, the battle may be the most action-packed you've ever experienced.

Snagging is very controversial. It is illegal in many areas and restricted to certain seasons, certain waters, certain fish and certain types of tackle in many others.

There is growing sentiment to stop snagging entirely in some areas where it is practiced. Many people believe it is an unsportsmanlike method for catching fish and that excessive numbers of fish are being harvested.

Studies done in areas where snagging is legal and popular do not support these contentions. For example, a survey conducted on two tailwaters on the Coosa River in Alabama found that "snagging catch rates were not excessive." Over a 3-month period during the peak spring snagging season, the daily catch by snaggers averaged only about 50 fish. That worked out to less than 1 fish per hour per snagger. Only 5 to 10 of those fish were catfish, and snaggers had to work several hours for each one caught. Snagging efforts and success dropped drastically during other seasons.

Is snagging unsportsmanlike? In the eyes of many, yes. In the eyes of others, definitely not. If any practice can be shown to threaten our fish resources, then, certainly, we have an obligation to restrict that practice. But in areas where it has been studied, snagging catfish does not fit that criterion.

5

SPECIAL
SITUATIONS

Thick Cover

On waters with little fishing pressure, thick cover might not hold any more large catfish than other, more easy-to-fish areas. But on heavily fished waters, there seems to be a definite correlation between big cats and woody tangles.

There are two reasons for this. First, catfish don't get big by frequenting heavily fished haunts. Most heavyweights get big by living in out-of-the-way places where most anglers don't dare to venture. That's why they haven't been caught already.

Second, big catfish instinctively prefer the protection of heavy cover. Outsized cats are extremely wary and angler-shy, which contributes to their natural tendency to hide in the most concealed places possible.

Cats in thick cover still accept an angler's offerings, but only on their terms. To be successful, you must be willing to make a slow, cautious, difficult entry into the flooded jungle.

Not every patch of thick cover holds big cats. The best provide easy movement between shallow and deep water. Look for brush piles, fallen trees, inundated willows and buckbrush, flooded timber and other dense woody cover along channel drop-offs, underwater humps and holes, the edges of shallow flats and other fast-breaking structure. Other hideouts hold big cats, too, but these are among the best.

GOOD LOCATIONS TO FIND CATFISH IN THICK COVER

•*Downed trees*, especially those found on the outside bend of a river, consistently hold catfish.

•*Logjams* create current breaks, which attract catfish looking for feeding sites and spawning cover.

•*Flooded brush* during high- water periods attracts crayfish and other forage, and catfish follow.

One hot spot to investigate is an outside river bend containing several downed trees. Outside bends generally have deep pockets of water adjacent to a channel break. Add the thick cover of branchy underwater treetops and you have an ideal cat hideout.

Heavy line and tackle are a must for this type of fishing. You don't want to let a hooked fish fiddle around in the cover. Get it out of there, as quick as you can, and let it do its fighting in open water. Use at least 20-pound-test line on a quality baitcasting reel, and a long, stout rod. Strong, abrasion-resistant line is a necessity when hossing big battlewise cats out of these hideaways. A long rod is best in this situation and accompishes two things: more leverage than a short rod to muscle a fish out of thick brush, and better accuracy to place a rig into dense thickets where casting is virtually impossible.

Be sure to set your drag just barely below your line's breaking point. You don't want a big brushpile cat peeling off any more line than necessary, or you'll be hung up in an instant.

If you're fishing from a boat, take along a big landing net, too, or better yet, a gaff hook, if you know you're going to keep your catch. It's tough getting a giant catfish in a boat under any circumstances, but a gaff or the right size net helps land a fish quicker, which means less chance of it making another powerful run for cover.

The best rig to use for fishing thick cover is a plain hook, unweighted. The size of the hook is determined by what type of bait you use. Weighted rigs can be used in certain situations, such as heavy current, but for the most part, they get tangled in cover more often than not.

TIPS FOR CATCHING CATS IN THICK COVER

USE a sturdy rod rigged with heavy line to catch cats out of heavy timber. Pull the line so the bait is snug against the rod tip, then work the bait into cover and drop it.

ANCHOR upstream of a snag and cast your rig just upstream of it. The current will carry the rig under the logs where catfish often hold.

Any standard catfish bait can be used, but for cats in thick cover, cut shad or carp are hard to beat. Big cats love cut-bait, and it won't tangle up like live minnows or crawfish. Thread a chunk about 2 inches square on a 3/0 hook, and unless current is strong, don't use any weight.

Now that you're properly armed and on the field of battle, you need to plan the logistics of your attack. Fact is, there's only one way to go about it: get right in there with them for close-quarters combat.

Get within rod's reach of the cover, and work slowly and precisely, moving your rig over, under and through the cover until you can ease it down into an opening. You can catch a few nice cats along the edge of the cover, but most are buried in it and strike only when the bait is right on their nose.

Allow the unweighted bait to sink into a likely looking hole or pocket. Keep dropping your rig into different pockets in the cover until it has been thoroughly fished. You don't need to wait in one pocket very long; an active cat should grab your bait soon after it is in front of him.

When a fish does strike, react immediately; set the hook hard, and reel like crazy. You must get a good hook set and pull the fish out of cover before it has time to tie you up. That's why heavy tackle is so important. This battle requires brawn, not finesse.

Another effective way to fish a brush pile or snag is with a slip-bobber rig. This way, there's less chance of getting snagged beneath the surface, and you can fish in and around cover effectively by controlling the drift of the rig in the current or wind.

Fluctuating Water Levels

Rising and falling water in a river or lake can have a dramatic influence on catfish activity. Under some conditions, cats move about like nomads, stuffing their guts to the point of bursting. In other situations, they settle in around current-breaking structure and wait for the food to come to them. There are no hard-and-fast rules, but it pays to know what catfish are likely to do when water levels fluctuate.

During a fast rise or fall, such as several inches a day, small catfish in rivers tend to concentrate in areas where they can escape the excessively heavy flow – scour holes, channel edges, inundated lakes and backwaters. Although sedentary, these catfish actively feed, and higher fish densities usually mean better catches for savvy cat fans who know where their quarry is likely to be holed up. To locate fish-holding structure, use a flasher or liquid crystal graph, then fish them using the appropriate drift-fishing or still-fishing techniques.

Big catfish don't behave like their smaller brethren in this situation. Being more powerful, they're not as affected by the fast-moving water. As a river starts to rise or fall, they go on a feeding spree that may carry them upstream and downstream through their home area several times in just a few hours. Many enter smaller tributaries and gorge on the smorgasbord of food items washed downstream. Others simply roam, and eat whatever happens by.

Except during flood conditions, this is a great time for bankfishing. Big cats are moving more, increasing the chance of one finding your bait. Use a three-way rig with a heavy sinker to keep the bait stationary yet visible off the bottom. And be sure you're properly equipped. This is one of the best times to hook a trophy-class flathead or blue. Don't lose one due to puny tackle that can't handle the strain.

Water-level fluctuations in big lakes and reservoirs tend to be less severe, thus they seldom have the dramatic influence on cat behavior found in rivers. Heavy rainfall, however, often triggers feeding frenzies that send catfish scurrying about in search of newly available food items.

In river-connected oxbows, the influence of rising and falling water is more noticeable. A fast rise scatters catfish. They seldom stay concentrated and hold around cover. Most suspend and randomly move around.

Drift-fishing with multiple rigs is the best option to locate and catch these fish during a fast rise. Set your rods so your baits run at different depths, then troll slowly, making large zigzagging sweeps. Troll over structure between normal resting and feeding areas. If you're patient and cover lots of water, sooner or later you'll catch fish.

A fast drop in water level moves catfish to deep-water haunts. Instinct moves them deeper until the water level stabilizes. Many fish suspend, holding tight to cover in a lake's midsection.

These catfish can be persnickety, often reluctant to bite. Still-fishing rigs work best on them, and you'll have to present your bait very close before they'll take it. Smaller baits work best in this situation – nightcrawlers, grape-sized chunks of cut-bait, small minnows, etc.

Fishing runout areas – the cuts connecting oxbow lakes and their parent rivers – also can be outstanding during a fast fall. Baitfish concentrate near these runouts, and catfish follow for an easy meal. A slip-bobber rig is the best choice here. Cast above the runout and guide the rig past brush and other current-breaking cover.

On oxbows that receive seasonal river overflows, catfish anglers should know the river-gauge level at which the parent river overflows into each oxbow. When gauge numbers are higher than this number, the river and oxbow are connected, and you must ascertain the intensity of water level fluctuations – fast rise, slow fall, etc. – to determine the best catfishing days. When gauge numbers are lower than the "magic" number, the river level is so low that it doesn't flow into the lake. Consequently, fishing conditions are more stable and predictable.

The best way to obtain the gauge number is to inquire at local baitshops or to ask area anglers. You can then read the current gauge number in local newspapers to plan a trip during peak periods.

The same applies to rivers. Watch newspapers or check government agency "hot lines" to determine what water conditions are, and what they're expected to be, before you go fishing.

PRIME LOCATIONS FOR CATFISH WHEN WATER LEVELS RISE AND FALL

•*Flooded trees* act as current breaks during high water, and hold schools of small fish and other creatures, which attract catfish.

•*Tributaries* often bring in water of a different temperature or clarity than the main lake or river, which attracts baitfish, and ultimately catfish.

•*Run-out areas* from oxbow lakes into the main river are super locations to catch catfish when the water is on a slow rise or fall.

Clear Water

If you're a swimmer, water skier or diver, you're probably thrilled when you can enjoy your pastime in a sparkling clear body of water. If you also enjoy catfishing, however, you also know clear water can be a despicable spoiler of angling fun. Clear water is the catfish angler's bane, and unless you know how to overcome the problems it presents, you can face many fishless hours.

Fishing clear waters presents special challenges for the catfish angler. Catfish in such a visible environment are especially cautious and respond differently to most factors than catfish living in stained or muddy water. Mistakes or miscalculations are not easily forgiven in clear waters.

Clear waters may be in ponds, streams, lakes, bayous or quarries. Many are drinking-water clear year-round; others clear up only during the low-rainfall periods of summer and winter. Spring rains and runoff, as well as the turbulence of fall turnover, tend to discolor the water during those times, but in between, the water becomes virtually gin clear.

Catfish rely heavily on sight to find their prey in clear water. They can see your offerings and readily chase moving baits. Light penetration is good, so weeds grow deeper, and oxygen is found farther down. Consequently, catfish are often found deeper as well.

Clear-water catfish shy away from periods of bright sunlight, favoring darker waters for ambushing food. During daylight hours, they are more likely to be in cover that provides shade or darkness. They feed more at night and around dawn and dusk, and tend to be more active on

165

cloudy, overcast days. Catfish also roam more in clear waters and are easily spooked by careless anglers.

When seeking clear-water catfish, the careful, quiet approach is usually most productive. Movements should be slow and deliberate. Take advantage of shoreline cover for camouflage. Wear shades of light blue or gray to help you blend in with the sky. Only your bait, not you, should be seen by the catfish.

Fishing during low-light periods is the key to success on many clear waters. The fish are generally more active at this time, and you minimize the problem of spooking fish before you can hook one. Catfish often move into shallow water areas to feed in the early morning and late afternoon, when light penetration is minimal. Cloudy days can mean many hours of successful catfishing, and during the heat of summer, many catfish fans have their best bite after dark.

It's difficult to catch clear-water catfish when fishing too close. Long casts are important, so it's best to fish with light line and long rods that allow you to toss a bait some distance.

One way successful catfish anglers cope with clear water is to fish deep. No matter how clear the water may seem, it still cuts light penetration, and at a depth of 20 feet or more, light is sufficiently reduced that it doesn't disturb catfish. In extreme cases, light penetration may extend 30 feet or more, and catfish drop to even deeper water to escape the harsh rays of the sun, being restricted in their vertical migration only by the constraints of oxygen.

To fish deep-water areas, cast fast-sinking baits from a distance. Or position your boat over structure to work a bait using a vertical "lift-drop" presentation.

QUICK TIP: Use a fluorocarbon leader when fishing finicky cats in clear water. This type of line is less visible in water than regular mono-filament, but just as strong.

If deep-water angling isn't your cup of tea, don't fret. You can catch catfish in shallow water if you locate shady cover. Virtually anything that casts a shadow is potentially productive, though objects that provide shade throughout the entire day are best. Boat docks are among the

166

best clear-water catfishing hot spots, especially those built close to the water's surface. Dense stands of flooded timber and logs are also good, as are thick beds of lily pads, man-made brush piles or "fish attractors," hollow cypress trees, flooded thickets, channels beneath bridges, underwater ledges and back ends of wooded coves.

Often the best approach is to avoid clear water and find water with a bit of tint. Large lakes or reservoirs usually offer water somewhere with a little color. This can often be found where tributaries dump in dirtier water or current stirs up bottom debris. This same current also cuts light penetration by rippling the surface of the water. Wind provides the same service but is decidedly less reliable.

QUICK TIP: Look for a mudline on the windy shoreline of a clear lake. The wave action pounding on shore often creates a dirty water area, which draws baitfish and feeding catfish.

Catfish usually aren't line shy, but in clear-water situations, lighter lines offer several advantages. First, with lighter line, you gain extra yardage on your casts. This helps you maintain more distance from your fishing area so catfish aren't spooked by shadows or movements. Second, smaller-diameter lines have less resistance in water, so your bait sinks quicker, hurrying to the depths where catfish are likely to be. Finally, light lines aren't as likely to be noticed by unusually spooky catfish, thus increasing your chances of a successful hookup.

Cold Water

Many anglers think catfish are inactive in cold water. That's only partially true. Blue and channel catfish feed actively throughout winter in most waters. Occasional catches by ice fishermen provide the most noteworthy evidence of this. Flathead catfish, on the other hand, become lethargic in cold water. Food habit studies indicate very little winter feeding. They become essentially inactive when water temperatures drop below 45°F and rarely take a bait unless it's placed right under their nose.

To catch channel cats and blues consistently in cold water, it helps to understand their winter feeding patterns.

One such pattern involves winter-killed shad. Gizzard and threadfin shad, two primary catfish forage items, are intolerant of severe cold. When the water temperature dips below 45°F, both species become cold-stressed. If the cold persists and the water temperature continues dropping, many of the shad die. This phenomenon, a yearly event on many first-rate cat waters, is known as winterkill.

When winterkill starts, catfish flock around shad schools like buzzards around a roadkill. They gorge themselves on these dead and dying baitfish to the point of bursting. This pattern may last a day or a month, depending on the weather. But while it lasts, fishing for big blues and channels is at its best.

To capitalize on this cold-weather pattern, use sonar to pinpoint schooling shad, then throw a cast net over the school to collect your bait. Large shad can be sliced for cut-bait, but small whole shad (an inch or two long) work best. Hook two or three on a single hook, running the hook through the eyes and leaving the barb exposed. Now lower your rig through the school of baitfish to the bottom, reel it up about a foot, and hang on. If the winterkill feeding frenzy is in full swing, mere seconds pass before a catfish strikes and the fight begins.

Be sure to keep plenty of shad ready for rigging. Where one cat is caught, there usually are dozens. Don't be caught without bait when the bite is on.

Freshwater mussels are another of the catfish's favorite winter foods. These mollusks live in dense colonies or *beds*. In winter, blue cats and channels congregate around these beds where they feed day after day with little expenditure of energy. Beds are usually

> QUICK TIP: Locate shad schools with a graph or flasher, then look for catfish below them. Lower a bait right on top of them.

near shore in 3 to 6 feet of water. They can be pinpointed during low-water periods or found by moving parallel to shore and probing the bottom with a cane pole. Catfish return to the same beds season after season, so once a bed is found, memorize its location or mark it on a map.

A slip-sinker rig is ideal for fishing around mussel beds. Use mussel flesh for bait, or small chunks of cut shad or herring. Although the catfish may be feeding mainly on mussels, they won't pass up a piece of cut-bait that's properly presented.

Cast to the shell beds you've found, and let your bait sit on the bottom undisturbed for up to 15 minutes. If no bite is forthcoming, move to another spot and try again. If you catch a cat, fish the water for several yards in either direction. It's likely others are feeding in the area as well.

The coldest weeks of winter may bring on a period of reduced feeding activity as the water temperature reaches its lowest extreme. As the water nears freezing, a catfish's metabolism drops dramatically, and very little food is needed to maintain a healthy state. This does not mean, however, that catfish cease to feed altogether. The lower level of metabolism simply permits the fish to survive if

QUICK TIP: Hook three or four small shad or other baitfish on a single hook when fishing below a shad school. This imitates dying shad.

food supplies are scarce, and anything that can be eaten without an undue expenditure of energy, including the angler's bait, is still gobbled up.

During this period, you may have to use sonar to pinpoint individual fish, then lower a bait very close to them in order to entice a strike. Most of these cats lay right on the bottom, sometimes partially covered by silt and mud. In rivers and ponds, look for them congregated in the deepest holes. There may be hundreds in a spot no larger than an acre. In reservoirs, look for winter schools around creek and river channel drop-offs, powerplant discharges, humps and inundated lakes and ponds. Cut-bait fished using a vertical presentation is ideal in all these situations.

Cats Under the Ice

MOST CATFISHERMEN in the North put away their cat rods in late fall when ice starts forming on lakes and rivers, and don't even think about catfish until spring. What most don't realize is that channel catfish can be caught all winter long through the ice.

Ice fishermen targeting walleyes and other gamefish on lakes and rivers also containing catfish are often surprised when the big fish they're fighting comes through the hole and has whiskers.

Savvy anglers are deliberately fishing for channel cats all winter and having success at it. The key is finding a body of water with a good population of catfish, and locating a deep hole where they're wintering. Once found, all that is needed is a 1/8- to 1/4-ounce jig head and a piece of cut sucker or other baitfish. Rig this on a quality ice rod spooled with 8-pound line and you're set to go.

Another helpful item is a portable flasher. This helps you find the proper water and lets you know if there is a fish staring at your bait so you don't pull it away.

Winter catfish are not the aggressive biters they are in summer, so don't work the bait too fast.

Deep Water

Look deep. That's the first rule of midsummer catfishing on big, deep lakes, especially during daylight hours. Many anglers expect catfish to be in the same shallow-water haunts where they roamed during the late-spring/early summer spawning period. Fishermen stubbornly fish near-shore structure and cover throughout summer and don't catch anything but squirts after bigger fish come off their beds. In reality, the biggest catfish have moved to deep "bluewater" areas – those places in a body of water offering the most favorable levels of water temperature and oxygen.

To master this deep-water catfishing, you need to first understand why cats move to deep water. In summer, many lakes stratify into three layers, because they are too deep for wave action to thoroughly mix the water. The warmest, oxygen-rich water stays on top: the cold, dense oxygen-free water settles on the bottom, and a middle layer of cool, oxygen-rich water called the *thermocline* forms in between. The thermocline is the zone of water where the temperature drops very fast. Of the three layers, the thermocline best satisfies the fishes' needs for dissolved oxygen and water temperature, and is also where the baitfish are. Rivers, on the other hand, never stratify because the water is constantly moving and stays mixed from top to bottom.

The depth and thickness of the thermocline varies from one body of water to another. In smaller lakes, it may be 10 feet down and only a foot thick; in extremely large, deep lakes, it may be 30 feet down and several feet thick.

Regardless of its location and size, the thermocline is where most sizable catfish are during periods of temperature extremes. And though the thermocline doesn't occupy the deepest part of the lake, it's still far deeper than the thin layer of surface water most catfish anglers fish.

The key is being able to locate the thermocline. You can accomplish this using one of two methods. A submersible temperature gauge shows you, by degree, exactly where the thermocline is. Or, you can use a liquid crystal graph to locate the correct depth. On many locators, the thermocline shows up as a foggy band across the screen. Sensitive units pick up this layer because the water is more dense at the thermocline. Even if the thermocline doesn't show up on your equipment, you'll still notice the bulk of the fish are suspended in a distinct band of water. That is the thermocline, or at least the depth zone you are looking for. Begin fishing at that depth.

If you have a liqiud crystal graph, try to locate cover or structure in the thermocline where catfish might concentrate – a channel drop-off, an underwater hump, the edge

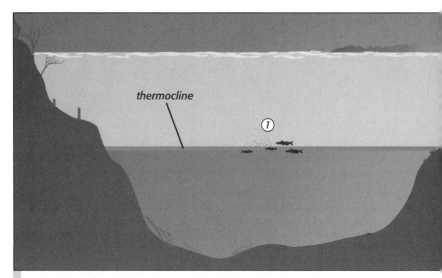

STRATIFICATION of a lake or reservoir occurs during extended periods of hot weather and causes most fish, including catfish, to change locations according to temperature and oxygen levels. Key spots to find catfish when this happens include: (1) the thermocline, especially near

of an inundated pond, deep weedbeds or perhaps a cluster of tall stumps beneath the surface. If you don't have a depth sounder, look for topside features that may continue underwater to the desired depth – bridge or dock pilings, long, steeply sloping points, rocky ledges, toppled trees or the outside edge of a weedbed. Once you've found such areas, you're ready to fish.

A bell sinker bottom rig is the best choice for taking bottom-feeding catfish in areas where the thermocline touches the lakebed. Add your favorite bait – worms, chicken liver and cut-bait are excellent choices – then cast the rig and let it sit on the bottom.

If fish seem persnickety, do away with the sinker altogether. Without any weight, a piece of bait sinks very slowly, providing an almost irresistible allurement for bluewater catfish. Watch the line very closely as the bait sinks, looking for any slight movement indicating a hit.

If catfish are suspended, try fishing bait under a slip-bobber rig (p. 93). This way, you can fish your bait at the same level as the thermocline, merely by adjusting the bobber

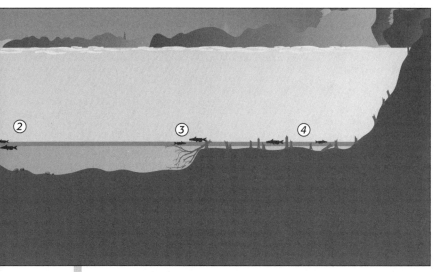

schools of baitfish, (2) midlake humps that touch the thermocline, (3) sunken timber on a drop-off that extends into the thermocline and (4) timbered flats that are not below the thermocline.

stop to the proper depth.

Bobber watchers may have to get used to fishing suspended fish, because cats often come up for the bait, and the float rises in the water column or sits on its side when the bait is taken. Set the hook when this happens, or risk having the hook inhaled into the catfish's nether reaches.

Another good way to catch suspended cats is by drift-fishing (p. 128). Keep your baits near the themocline and cover lots of water, either by drifting with the wind or using an electric trolling motor. Once you find fish, work the area thoroughly, as cats often school up around large pods of baitfish.

Inundated creek and river channels are among the most common types of structure where deep-water cats are found. Use a flasher or graph to help pinpoint fish concentrated in these areas. Among the specific spots to check in the main body of a lake are those where feeder creeks merge with river channels. Check the water on the two points created by the juncture of the two streams, and for several yards in all directions, up the feeder stream, and up and down the river channel.

QUICK TIPS: Find the thermocline using a hand-held temperature gauge. Note the depth where the sharp drop in temperature occurs.

Look for schools of baitfish on the locator at a certain level. This is usually the depth of the thermocline.

Secondary creek channels can also be prolific catfish producers. Look for those in or near the thermocline that offer sharp breaklines and ledges or drop-offs.

Deep-water catfish, especially blues and channels, are often found in loose schools. When you find one, others are likely to be nearby. You'll increase your catch rate if you make a concerted effort to work your bait thoroughly around each piece of cover.

Trophy Cats

How big is a trophy catfish? That depends on several things – where you fish, the type of catfish you're seeking, maybe even how big a catfish you've caught before. Generally speaking, however, any channel cat over

20 pounds is an exceptional fish, and for most anglers, a flathead or blue over 50 would be the trophy of a lifetime.

Trophy catfish inhabit many waters, but few anglers challenge them with rod and reel on a regular basis. Few know how to do it, and fewer still possess the persistence to be successful. Trophy-class catfish may be older than the anglers who seek them, and with each passing year, they become more elusive. Catching these monsters may be the greatest challenge in freshwater fishing. It is possible, though, and you can soon catch a trophy if you keep the following things in mind.

First, don't bother fishing for trophy catfish unless you have lots of patience. Catching one doesn't happen every day, even for those familiar with their daily habits. As one avid catfish angler put it, "Fishin' for giant cats is like trophy muskie fishing, only lonelier." You may spend days or weeks trying to pinpoint a single trophy fish. And as the hours pass, the doubts begin to grow, and you start wondering if it's worth it.

That's why many anglers give up trophy catfishing even before they land their first big fish; they don't have enough patience.

Learn to bide your time without getting frustrated. Bring a comfortable seat, plenty of cold drinks and snacks, a can of bug spray, and a buddy to talk to. It could be a long night. Maybe several long nights. But sooner or later, the patient catter reaps his reward.

Persistence is equally important, says Randle Hall, a trophy cat guide from Corinth, Texas.

"Anyone can learn the tactics necessary for catching cats," he notes. "You learn that you have to change the places you fish and what you fish and how you fish from day to day as weather and other conditions dictate. But to catch a trophy-class fish, you have to keep bait in the water where the big ones swim. Learn all you can about a lake or river where you know those big fish are. Then stay at it, day after day, learning more. Catfishermen who do that have the best chance of catching a trophy, maybe even a world record."

Another tip: focus your efforts on large rivers and lakes. Trophy cats seldom come from creeks, ponds and small lakes. It happens occasionally, but not often enough to merit your attention. When seeking a true heavyweight, focus on sizable bodies of water.

Invest in good heavy tackle, and maintain it in good condition. Joe Drose of Cross, South Carolina, one of the world's top trophy catfish guides, has this to say about catching trophy cats.

"The tactics and rigs you use probably aren't as important as the preparation," he says. "Any time you're fishing water where big catfish live, there's a chance Godzilla's gonna bite. You have to be ready for him every time you go out there, or he'll find a way to get the best of you.

"You should only fish with good tackle – high-quality rods, reels, line and so forth. And pay attention to details all the time. For instance, be sure to change your fishing line regularly, and check it every time you catch a fish to see if it's scarred up and needs to be replaced. I figure lots and lots of folks have hooked world-record-class catfish, but they simply weren't prepared to land them. A guy will think, 'Gee, I should have changed that leader.' But he doesn't do it. He throws it out there anyway. And wham! The next world record hits. It rolls and wraps up in the line and suddenly that leader snaps where it's scarred. The fish is gone, and the guy is heart-broken. If only he'd taken a minute to replace that leader, he might have caught the fish of a lifetime.

"Bottom line is, you've got to be prepared before you hook that fish, and know exactly what to do after you hook it. If not, you don't stand a chance."

Be picky about the bait you use, too. Trophy-class cats rarely are caught using chicken liver, stinkbaits, catalpa worms, cheese and other things that small cats frequently eat. Baitfish are your best bet – live ones for flatheads, and either live or cut-bait for big channels and blues.

Trophy cat seekers also should know how to properly play and land a big fish. Heavyweight cats don't give up easily, and even if you hook one, that's no guarantee you'll get it on the dry side of a boat.

Don't fight a fish with the reel. Play it with your arms and the rod. Point the rod straight up, and allow the bend of the rod to tire the fish. Hold your ground while the catfish is fighting; then, when it eases up, lower your rod tip toward

---

WATERS FOR TROPHY CATFISH

Your first step to catching a huge cat is fishing water that grows trophies. The list below shows you where to go, when to go and what you can expect to catch once you're there.

Clear Lake, **California – channels, warm months**

Irvine Lake, **California – blues and channels, year-round**

Brownlee Reservoir, **Idaho & Oregon – flatheads, warm months**

Cochiti Lake, **New Mexico – channels, year-round**

Choke Canyon Reservoir, **Texas – channels, blues and flatheads, year-round**

Toledo Bend Lake, **Texas and Louisiana – flatheads, summer**

Lake Livingston, **Texas – blues, flatheads, channels, year-round**

Lake Lewisville, **Texas – flatheads, warm months**

Lake Thunderbird, **Oklahoma – flatheads, warm months**

Sherman Reservoir, **Nebraska – channels and flatheads, summer**

Red River, **North Dakota and Manitoba – channels, May and June**

Lake Texoma, **Oklahoma and Texas – blues, year-round**

Pomona Reservoir, **Kansas – flatheads, warm months**

Truman Lake, **Missouri – blues and flatheads, year-round**

Lower Mississippi River **(below St. Louis, Missouri) – blues, channels, flatheads, year-round**

---

the water, reeling on the drop. Be patient, and don't apply unneeded pressure.

Be sure your drag is set at a point just below the breaking strength of your line. Then, when a cat makes a run, the drag gives line. You may spend many days fishing before you finally hook a giant cat. If you get spooled or your line snaps, all that work was for nothing.

If you place your rod in a holder, be sure it's firmly anchored. Likewise, keep a firm grip on hand-held equipment. A big cat can yank a rod and reel into the water quicker than you can say, "Boo."

Keep a big, sturdy landing net handy, too. It's nearly impossible to land a giant catfish with your hands. Get it in a net, or risk losing it. Avoid nets with thin-walled aluminum handles; they'll buckle under the weight of a big cat.

Missouri River, **Missouri** – *blues, year-round*

Osage River, **Missouri** – *blues, year-round*

Lake Conway, **Arkansas** – *flatheads, summer months*

Arkansas River, **Arkansas** – *blues and flatheads, year-round*

Millwood Lake, **Arkansas** – *channels, blues and flatheads, year-round*

Nolin River Lake, **Kentucky** – *flatheads, warm months*

Lake des Allemands, **Louisiana** – *blues and flatheads, warm months*

Wheeler Lake, **Alabama** – *blues, year-round*

Tennessee River, **Tennessee** – *channels and blues, year-round*

Lake Tom Bailey, **Mississippi** – *channels, warm months*

Thurmond Lake, **Georgia** – *blues and flatheads, year-round*

Lakes Marion & Moultrie, **South Carolina** – *blues, channels and flatheads, year-round*

Lake Arthur, **Pennsylvania** – *channels, summer*

Claytor Lake, **Virginia** – *channels and flatheads, warm months*

Cape Fear River, **North Carolina** – *blues and flatheads, warm months*

Lake Seminole, **Georgia & Florida** – *flatheads, warm months*

Escambia River, **Florida** – *blues and flatheads, year-round*

If you know you're going to keep a big cat, a gaff hook is great for handling a fish that might be too large for a net.

When you finally land your first trophy catfish, take great pride in the fact that you've managed to triumph over one of freshwater fishing's finest trophies. Catch your second and third, and you enter a fraternity of elite anglers.

BAIT FOR CATCHING TROPHY CATFISH

•*Cut-bait* works best for blue and channel catfish. Use big chunks of shad, herring and other oily baitfish.

•*Live bait* is the most productive bait for catching trophy flathead catfish. For big fish, the larger, the better. Suckers, chubs and other fish 10 to 14 inches long are best.

Catfish Conservation

Many catfish anglers believe it's impossible to hurt a catfish population with hook and line. They're wrong. Heavy angling pressure can have a dramatic effect on catfish populations if it's not tempered by conservation. Big catfish are especially vulnerable, because once these ancients are removed, it takes years to replace them.

Take flatheads, for instance. Even though they're considered fast growing, in prime waters it takes 10 years for one to reach 30 pounds. The big ones – 60 pounds and up – are rare individuals that may have lived 30 years or more. Remove a trophy flathead from a river or lake, and it might be your elder. Chances are, it may not be replaced by a fish of similar size during your lifetime.

Unfortunately, research indicates that flathead anglers release less than 2 percent of their catch. Increased fishing pressure combined with a "take-'em-home-and-eat-'em" philosophy is making big flatheads harder and harder to find in many waters.

The same is true for channel and blue catfish. Trophy fish are old, uncommon fish. Yet many catfish anglers never consider releasing any of the fish they catch, especially big ones.

As more and more anglers join the catfishing fraternity, it becomes increasingly important for us to be conservation-minded anglers. If we aren't, we may lose many of the outstanding trophy fisheries that now exist. But that doesn't mean every catfish has to be released. If harvested wisely, there should be plenty of catfish to keep and eat. It's important, however, that we're selective about our harvest.

Small cats are more numerous than big ones, so if you're fish hungry, keep some of the smaller guys to eat. Try to resist the temptation to keep the big heavyweights. Shoot some photos for memory's sake, then carefully release the fish. Voluntary catch-and-release is a good way to protect and perpetuate our outstanding trophy catfishing opportunities.

Be sure to do it right. Catfish are extremely hardy. An individual may live for hours out of the water. But if you expect a cat to survive following release, it's important to handle it properly. Follow these simple tips, and you can greatly increase the chances the fish you turn back lives to be caught again.

•Use barbless hooks, or crimp the barbs with pliers.

•Bring the fish to the boat quickly; don't play it to total exhaustion while attempting to land it.

•Hold the fish in the water as much as possible when handling it, removing the hook and preparing it for release.

•Wet your hands before handling the fish to avoid removing its protective slime layer.

•If the fish has swallowed the hook, don't pull it out. Rather, cut the line as close to the hook as possible, leaving it inside the fish.

•Don't squeeze the fish or put your fingers in its gills. Cradle it in the water and move it back and forth to oxygenate the gills. When the fish is properly rested, it will swim from your hands.

Catfishermen have other obligations, too. It's important that we all work together to keep our lakes and rivers clean.

Show respect and consideration for other people who use those resources. We need to set a good example for others to follow, and leave positive images of catfishermen for those who don't fish or who fish for other species. Here are some tips that may help.

•Read your local fishing regulations booklet cover to cover this year, and stick by the rules – all the rules – year-round. Obtain the proper licenses. Obey creel and possession limits. Use only legal equipment and methods of harvest.

•If you fish with jugs, trotlines, limblines or yo-yos, take them with you when you leave. These items are a major form of unsightly garbage on our nation's catfishing waters and can be extremely dangerous to boaters, swimmers and wildlife.

•Properly dispose of used fishing line. Thousands of animals die yearly after becoming entangled in carelessly discarded line. Other trash is unsightly and sometimes dangerous, too – bait boxes, minnow bags, hook containers, broken bobbers, drink cans and leftover pieces of cut-bait. Don't drop any trash in the water or on shore. Take it with you for proper disposal at home.

•Avoid purposely introducing catfish in public waters where they aren't native. And don't discard unused live bait in the waters you fish. If an unwanted species gains a foothold, it can wreak havoc on natural ecosystems.

•When wading, disturb the streambed as little as possible to protect the delicate habitats there.

•Avoid spilling fuel and oil when filling your motor. These chemicals are deadly to aquatic life.

•Discuss the importance of being a responsible angler with your sons and daughters who fish. Explain your personal code of ethics, and encourage them to "do the right thing" when enjoying the outdoors.

By following these principles of conduct each time you go fishing, you give your best to the sport, the public, the environment and yourself. And believe it or not, actions really do speak louder than words.

TIPS FOR RELEASING TROPHY CATFISH

•*Flatten* the barb of a hook, or use barbless varieties for quick and easy removal from a catfish's jaw.

•*Keep* a large fish you plan on releasing in the water as long as possible. Remove it briefly for a quick picture, then return it to the water.

•*Use* a landing net made with soft, small mesh, such as a salmon net. This kind of net is easier on the smooth skin of a catfish than other nets.

Conserving What We Have

IN SOME STATES, catfish still are considered rough fish and you can legally keep as many as you want. Commercial fishing is also unregulated in many areas. On two of the country's most famous trophy catfish lakes, for instance, commercial anglers are allowed to use trotlines to catch cats. As long as they buy the proper tags, anglers can use up to 2,000 hooks. It's not unusual to see a commercial fisherman unloading a boat containing 100 30-pound catfish.

Unfortunately, facts such as these lead many anglers to believe that harvest restrictions and length limits are unnecessary. If the state says it's OK, then there must be plenty of catfish to support such practices. Right?

At one time, our country's bass anglers were asking the same question. Most of them used hit-and-miss fishing tactics, just as most of today's catfish anglers do. And bass seemed a limitless resource.

Enter the modern age of bass fishing. Around the early 1970s, a wide variety of sophisticated fishing equipment suddenly became available to the average bass angler. They also were flooded with more and more information on how to catch bass – in magazines and books, on TV, on videos. All this enabled bass fishermen to become more skillful and efficient.

As bassing became more and more popular, we learned that sport fishermen could adversely impact the quality of fishing by removing too many fish. Catch-and-release fishing, once scorned, quickly became the norm. Under pressure from sport fishermen, states started implementing more restrictive harvest regulations to protect and enhance our bass fisheries.

Now it's unusual to find a body of water that doesn't have a variety of harvest restrictions – length limits, catch-and-release only, etc.

Catfishing is a similar crossroads. The day is coming soon when many more catfishermen consistently catch more fish. With the rising popularity of the sport the need for voluntary and mandatory harvest restrictions will become necessary. The question is, will fisheries managers and catfishermen apply the lessons learned from the past before catfish populations are harmed?

To a large extent, the answer to that question depends on you. Changes won't be realized until catfishermen actively work to bring them about. You can help by contacting your elected and appointed representatives and communicating your concerns. Catfish are among the most popular sport fish in the nation, and properly managed sport fisheries can generate millions of dollars for a state's economy.

We should all work together to conserve this precious resource. If we don't, that which we take for granted may someday be gone.

Cleaning Catfish

After the fun of catfishing has subsided, anglers are faced with cleaning their catch. Some hire the job done, others suffer through the process, and still others, with a little know-how, accomplish it with relative ease.

Catfish should be skinned, regardless of their size. Two basic tools are required: A sharp knife and a good set of skinning pliers. A regular set of pliers works, but skinning pliers work much better because the jaws are wider, affording a better grip on the catfish's thin, slippery skin.

Some anglers also use a skinning board clamp or a board with a nail driven through it to hold the head in place. Large fish may have to be hung from a tree limb or other overhead support to facilitate cleaning. Small fish can be hand-held. Regardless of how you secure the fish, take care to avoid the sharp pectoral and dorsal spines throughout the cleaning process. If necessary, stun the fish with a hammer before you start skinning.

CATFISH CONTAMINANTS

Many waters harbor contaminants that are transferred to fish. In several states, health agencies have issued advisories regarding consumption of catfish from monitored waters. Sometimes people are advised to eat no catfish at all. In other cases, limited consumption is advised or particular groups of people (children and pregnant women, for instance) are cautioned not to eat catfish. Catfish anglers should check with state health agencies for advisories on waters being fished.

Unfortunately, many waters aren't monitored. Unsuspecting anglers could be at risk if catfish are consumed frequently or in large quantities. Fortunately, the health risk associated with consumption of fish containing trace amounts of most contaminants can be substantially reduced during cleaning. Skin and fillet all fish. The belly flap and the fatty strip along the backbone (backstrap) should be discarded, as well as all dark reddish meat along the lateral line (shaded areas in diagram). Broiling, baking or grilling fish provides additional risk reduction.

HOW TO SKIN AND FILLET CATFISH

1. MAKE a cut through the skin behind the head. Start behind the pectoral fin on one side of the fish, and cut up, over and down to the other pectoral fin.

2. USE the point of the knife to split the skin down the middle of the back, from head to tail, running down one side of the dorsal fin.

3. SPLIT the skin on the other side of the dorsal fin, connecting this cut to the one just made. The fish is now ready for skinning.

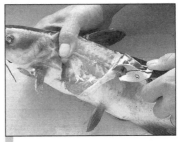

4. GRASP the skin with pliers and pull toward the tail. It should strip off in one or two pieces. Repeat the process on the other side.

5. REMOVE the meat along each side of the fish with a fillet knife. Cut around the rib cage for a totally boneless fillet.

6. CUT away all dark red flesh along the lateral line. This meat often harbors contaminants found in water and can have a strong flavor.

HOW TO CLEAN A CATFISH FOR WHOLE PANFRYING

AFTER skinning (p. 185), sever backbone just behind the head, using a heavy serrated knife or cleaver.

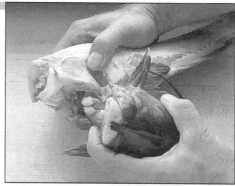

Pull the head away from the body (right, top). The pectoral fins and entrails should come with the head. Slice off the adipose fin and tail.

Remove the dorsal and anal fins by gripping each at its rear edge with skinning pliers and lifting toward the head of the fish (right).

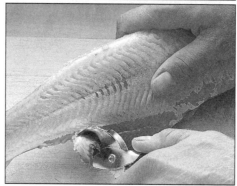

OTHER CLEANING TIPS

SAVE the belly flesh of a large catfish by stripping the belly skin toward the head, then cutting away the boneless meat. This meat is fatty but delicious.

MAKE steaks out of large catfish that have been dressed for panfrying. A whole fish of this size would take too long to cook properly.

Cooking Tips & Recipes

The delicate white flesh of catfish is delicious and easy to prepare. With many cooks, it's into the frying pan, onto the platter, don't spare the salt and pepper, and pass the ketchup. Even so, the way you fix catfish is limited only by your imagination.

The most important rule in preparing catfish is never overcook it. Catfish is naturally tender and cooks quickly. It's done when it flakes easily when tested with a fork. Cook it too long, and it becomes dry and tough. Remember, too, that the shorter the time from hook to cook, the better the flavor.

As with other fish, the catfish's flavor can vary according to the quality of water from which it came. Fish from polluted waters sometimes have a strong, objectionable taste, but if you catch cats in clean water, put them on ice soon after being caught, and dress them properly, they'll provide the entrée for many delicious meals. This is true even for bullheads.

The following recipes offer a variety of ways to add the delectable flavor of catfish to your menus.

CAJUN BATTERED CATFISH

2 to 3 pounds catfish fillets or steaks
1 cup prepared mustard
2 eggs, slightly beaten
1 teaspoon Louisiana hot sauce
1/2 cup corn flour
1/2 cup cornmeal
1/2 cup all-purpose flour
1/2 cup dried Italian bread crumbs
1 teaspoon salt
1 teaspoon garlic powder
1 teaspoon freshly ground black pepper
1 teaspoon paprika

In a bowl, combine mustard, eggs and hot sauce. In another bowl, combine the remaining ingredients, except catfish. Brush catfish with mustard mixture until well coated; dip fish in the dry mixture. Fry fish until golden brown in canola oil heated to 375°F.

Per Serving: Calories: 671 • Protein: 54 g. • Carbohydrate: 53 g. • Cholesterol: 238 mg. • Sodium: 1972 mg.

RALPH'S THREE RIVERS CATFISH

1 to 2 pounds catfish fillets
Salt to taste
2 cups self-rising cornmeal
1 cup self-rising flour
1 teaspoon garlic salt

1 teaspoon black pepper
1 tablespoon Lawry's Hot & Spicy
   seasoning salt
Vegetable or peanut oil

Salt the fillets to taste. Mix cornmeal, flour, garlic salt, black pepper and seasoning salt. Dredge fillets in this batter mix, and cook until golden brown in oil heated to 375°F. Serve Ralph-style with plenty of beer dogs, fried potatoes, thick-sliced tomatoes and onions, and homemade pickles.

Per Serving: Calories: 556 • Protein: 46 g. • Carbohydrate: 43 g.
• Cholesterol: 132 mg. • Sodium: 1565 mg.

PANFRIED CATFISH DILLY

6 small catfish, pan-dressed
4 tablespoons butter
4 tablespoons fresh chopped dill
1/2 cup flour

1/2 cup cornmeal
1 teaspoon salt
1 teaspoon freshly ground black
   pepper

Melt butter in a skillet, and add dill. Dredge fish in a mixture of flour, cornmeal, salt and pepper. Sauté in dill butter until done.

Per Serving: Calories: 480 • Protein: 43 g. • Carbohydrate: 17 g. •
Cholesterol: 173 mg. • Sodium: 688 mg.

CATFISH STEW WITH ONION, LEEK & GARLIC

3 tablespoons butter or margarine
1 cup finely chopped onion
1 leek, white part only, thinly
   sliced
1 clove garlic, minced
2 cups chicken broth
2 medium tomatoes, peeled,
   seeded and diced
2 tablespoons chopped fresh
   parsley

1 celery rib, finely chopped
1 bay leaf
1/4 teaspoon dried thyme
1/2 teaspoon freshly ground
   black pepper
1 cup dry white wine
1/2 pound catfish fillets, cut into
   bite-size pieces
1/4 pound shrimp, shelled
1/4 pound scallops
   dried dill

Heat the butter in the bottom of a large pot, and sauté onion, leek and garlic until soft. Add all other ingredients, except the catfish and shellfish. Mix well, and bring to a boil. Reduce heat and simmer, covered, for 10 minutes. Add catfish, shrimp and scallops, and cook until they turn opaque white, about 5 minutes. Garnish each bowl of stew with a sprinkle of dill.

Per Serving: Calories: 296 • Protein: 22 g. • Carbohydrate: 13 g.
• Cholesterol: 100 mg. • Sodium: 728 mg.

DIXIE CATFISH CHOWDER

1/2 cup chopped onion
2 tablespoons melted butter
1 pound catfish fillets, cut in
  bite-size pieces
2 cups diced potatoes
1 cup boiling water

1 teaspoon salt
1/2 teaspoon freshly ground
  black pepper
2 cups whole milk
1 (8³/4-oz.) can cream-style
  corn

Sauté onion in butter until soft. Add fish, potatoes, water, salt and black pepper. Cover and simmer for 15 minutes or until potatoes are tender. Add milk and corn; heat thoroughly, but do not boil. Serve piping hot.

Per Serving: Calories: 369 • Protein: 28 g. • Carbohydrate: 32 g. •
Cholesterol: 98 mg. • Sodium: 954 mg.

FAT CAT MULLIGAN

3 slices bacon, diced
3 medium onions, sliced thin
2 pounds catfish fillets, cut in
  bite-size pieces
2 pounds potatoes, diced
1/2 teaspoon celery seed
2 large carrots, diced
1/4 cup diced green bell pepper

1 tablespoon salt
2 teaspoons freshly ground
  black pepper
3 cups boiling water
3 1/2 cups chopped canned
  tomatoes
2 tablespoons fresh parsley,
  chopped fine

Sauté bacon in a deep kettle till lightly browned; remove bacon bits and set aside. Sauté onion slices in bacon grease until tender. Stir in fish, potatoes, celery seed, carrots, green pepper, salt, black pepper and water. Simmer, covered, until vege-tables are tender, about 30 minutes. Add tomatoes, and heat through. Garnish with chopped parsley and bacon bits.

Per Serving: Calories: 327 • Protein: 26 g. • Carbohydrate: 34 g. •
Cholesterol: 72 mg. • Sodium: 1191 mg.

BAKED BULLHEAD SUPREME

2 pounds bullhead fillets or
  pan-dressed bullheads
1/2 cup creamy French salad
  dressing

1 1/2 cups crushed cheese crackers
2 tablespoons melted butter or
  margarine
Paprika

Dip fillets in dressing, and dredge in cracker crumbs. Place on a well-greased baking sheet, and drizzle with melted butter. Season with paprika, and bake at 500°F for 10 to 12 minutes, or until fish flakes easily with a fork.

Per Serving: Calories: 658 • Protein: 47 g. • Carbohydrate: 26 g. •
Cholesterol: 147 mg. • Sodium: 1034 mg.

A

Age & Growth (charts),
  Of various bullheads, 40, 41
  Of various catfish, 19, 26, 32, 36
Aquaculture, 21

B

Baitfish,
  Collecting, 100, 101, 104, 105
  Fishing with, 84, 93, 94, 103-106,
    141, 149, 163, 169, 170, 177, 179
  In catfish diet, 16, 20, 25, 30, 37, 168
  Keeping alive, 100, 101, 104
Bait-Walker Rig, 87, 94
Barbels, 8, 12
Black Bullhead, 39, 40
  See also: Bullheads
Blood Bait, 112, 113
Blue Catfish, 22-27, 176
  Daily & seasonal activities, 25, 54, 168
  Distinguishing from other catfish,
    22, 23, 34, 35
  Fishing for, 93, 112
  Habitat, 25, 50, 51, 61
Boat,
  Drift-fishing, 129-134
  Still-Fishing, 120-124
Bobbers, 88, 89, 93
  Drift-fishing with, 134, 135
Bobby Pole, 149, 151
Bottom-Bouncer Rig, 87, 94, 95
Boulders, see: Rocks & Rocky Areas
Brackish Water, 37
Bridges & Pilings,
  Catfish locations, 52, 60, 63, 67
Brown Bullhead, 41
  See also: Bullheads
Brush, see: Timber & Brush
Bullheads,
  About & types, 38-41
  As catfish bait, 106, 149
  Distinguishing from catfish, 29, 34
  Fishing for, 112

C

Casting,
  Casting distance and rod length, 79
  Fan-casting, 74
Cast Net, 100 104, 105, 168
Catalpa Worms as Bait, 84, 103, 109,
  110, 146, 149

Catch-and-Release, 85, 115, 180-183
Channel Catfish, 18-21, 175
  Daily & seasonal activities, 20, 54, 168
  Distinguishing from other catfish,
    22, 23, 34, 35
  Fishing for, 93, 103, 112
  Habitat, 20, 50, 51, 54, 62
Chicken Liver as Bait, 20, 30, 114, 141
Chumming, 125
Chunk Bait, 116, 117, 141, 146
Clams, in catfish diet, 26
Clinch Knot, Improved, 96
Clouds, see: Rainy & Overcast Weather
Cold Water & Catfish Activity, 20, 25
Contaminants in Catfish Meat, 184
Crayfish,
  As bait, 85, 107, 108, 141, 149
  In catfish diet, 20, 26, 30, 31
Creeks, see: Rivers & Streams
Crustaceans in Catfish Diet, 37
  See also specific crustaceans
Current,
  Catfish preferences, 20, 25, 29, 36,
    54, 56
  Current seam, 52, 53, 55, 66
Cut-Bait, 84, 93, 103, 104, 111, 141,
  146, 149, 160, 163, 169, 177, 179

D

Daily Activities of Catfish, 20, 30
Dams,
  Catfish around, 53, 55, 61, 63, 74, 125
  Fishing techniques, 53, 62, 123, 125,
    126
Dead Bait, 103, 169
  See also: Cut-Bait
Deep-Water Fishing, 166, 171-174
Dip Bait, 115
  Recipe, 117
Doughbait, 85, 113, 114
  Recipes, 114, 117
Drift-Fishing Rigs, 92, 130
Dropper Loop Knot, 97
Dropper Loop Rig, 92

E

Electronics, 98, 99
Electrosensing, 16, 17

F

Farming of Catfish, 21
Filleting Catfish, 185

Fins of Catfish, 8
Fish Guts as Bait, 20, 85
Flathead Catfish, 28-33, 176
  Daily & seasonal activities, 30, 54, 168
  Distinguishing from bullheads, 29
  Fishing for, 93
  Habitat, 29, 50, 51, 60
Float Rigs, 93, 94, 130
Foods & Feeding,
  How catfish & bullheads locate
    food, 8, 13-15, 38
  In rivers & streams, 52, 61
  Of various bullheads, 38
  Of various catfish, 20, 25, 30, 37,
    103, 107, 108, 112, 168, 169
Frogs, 20, 110, 149

G
Gradient, 51
Gravel-Bottomed Areas, 25, 30, 58
Grocery Store Baits, 20, 26, 38, 114
Grooves below Dam, 61, 123, 125

H
Habitat Preferences,
  Of various bullheads, 40, 41
  Of various catfish, 20, 25, 29, 36
Handling Catfish, 127
Hard Bottomed Areas, 25
Herring, see: Baitfish
Hole in River Pool, 52, 55, 59
Hooks, 83-85

I
Ice Fishing, 170
Improved Clinch Knot, 96
Insects & Insect Larvae, 20, 26, 37

J
Jug Fishing, 101, 144-147

L
Landing Nets, 99
Lateral Line, 13, 15, 16
Leeches, 20, 58, 110, 111
Limbline Fishing, 85, 110, 148-151
Line, 81, 82, 149, 167
Locks, 61, 62
Logs & Logjams, see: Timber & Brush

M
Man-Made Lakes, 49, 64-67
  Catfish species in, 20, 37
  Water-level fluctuations, 129, 162-164
Mid-Water Structure, 66, 122, 133, 173
Mussels, 20, 108, 169

N
Natural Lakes, 49
  Bullhead species in, 40, 41
  Catfish species in, 36
Night,
  Catfish Activities, 20, 30, 36, 59
  Night fishing, 80, 82, 88, 141
Nightcrawlers, 84, 107, 146, 149, 163
Noodling, 152-155

O
Ocean Catfish, 43, 44
Oxbow Lakes, 68-71
  Catfish species in, 20
  Fishing techniques, 133, 162-164
Oxygen Levels, 73
  Catfish preferences, 20
  Bullhead preferences, 38, 40

P
Paddlefish, 45
Palomar Knot, 96
Paternoster Rig, 91, 94
Pencil-Lead Sinker Rig, 130, 132
Ponds, 49, 72-75
  Bullhead species in, 40, 41
  Catfish species in, 20, 37, 72
  Fishing techniques, 73, 74
  Flooded pond in man-made lake, 66
Pool in River, see: Rapids-Pool
Power Plant, 66

R
Rainy & Overcast Weather, 30, 59, 166
Rapids-Pool, 51, 52, 59
Recipes for Stinkbaits, 114, 117
Reels, 80, 81
Reservoirs, see: Man-Made Lakes
Riprap, 61, 63, 66, 71, 120, 133, 149
River Channel in Man-Made Lake, 64
Rivers & Streams, 49
  Big rivers, 56-63
  Bullhead species in, 40, 41
  Catfish species in, 20, 25, 29, 36, 50
  Equipment, 79, 87
  Fishing techniques, 122, 123, 149-151
  Small to mid-sized rivers, 50-55
  Water-level fluctuations, 129, 162-164
Rocks & Rocky Areas, 52, 53, 58
Rod Holders, 100
Rods, 78-80, 125

S
Salamanders, 20, 110, 149
Sandy Areas, 25, 30

Scour Hole, 53, 54
Seasonal Locations & Activities of Catfish, 67
Fall, 54, 62, 66, 67, 74
Spring, 62, 67, 74
Summer, 54, 59, 62, 66, 67, 70, 171
Winter, 25, 54, 62, 66, 70, 168-170
Senses of Catfish, 12-17
Compared to other gamefish, 14
Shad, see: Baitfish
Shoreline Fishing, 74, 122, 124-127, 163
Shoreline Structure, 52, 53, 72, 122, 124-127
Shrimp in Catfish Diet, 20
Sinkers, 85-87
Skin of Catfish,
Lack of scales, 8
Removing (cleaning), 185
Tastebuds on skin, 14, 15
Slip-Bobber Rig, 88, 89, 163, 173
Slip-Sinker Rig, 86, 90, 169
Snagging, 78, 154, 155
Spawning Activities,
Catfish locations, 65, 67
Of various bullheads, 38
Of various catfish, 20, 26, 32, 36, 44
Species of Catfish, 9, 10, 42-44
Spines in Catfish Fins, 8
Sponge Bait, 115
Stinkbait, 20, 30, 38, 112, 141, 149
Recipes, 117
Stocking,
Bullheads, 38
Catfish, 19, 20, 24, 26, 37, 48, 72
Stocking catfish to control other fish populations, 33
Streams, see: Rivers & Streams
Sunfish as Bait, 84, 93, 104, 149
Suspended Catfish, 74, 93, 173, 174
Swivels, 87

T
Tackle Boxes, 99, 100
Tailraces, 61, 62, 126
Talking Catfish, 10
Tapetum Lucidum, 16

Thermocline, 67, 171-174
Three-Way Rig, 86, 87, 91, 127
Timber & Brush,
Catfish around, 30, 52, 54, 55, 58, 64, 71, 164, 167, 173
Fishing techniques, 159-161
Tributaries, 59, 60, 63, 65, 164
Trolling Sinker Rig, 130, 131
Trotline Fishing, 84, 85, 101, 136-141
Baits for, 109, 110, 117, 141
How to make trotline rig, 137
Setting a trotline, 138, 139
Tube Bait, 116

W
Water Clarity,
Bullhead preferences, 38
Catfish preferences, 20, 25, 60
Fishing clear water, 165-167
Water Level Fluctuations, 70, 71
Fishing techniques, 129, 162-164
Water Temperature,
And catfish activity, 20, 25
Fishing cold water, 168-170
Weeds & Weedbeds,
Aquatic plants in catfish diet, 37
Bullheads around, 40
Catfish around, 71, 75, 167
Equipment for fishing, 85, 86
Fishing techniques, 158-161
White Catfish, 34-37
Distinguishing from other catfish, 34
Willow Trees, 71
Wing Dams, 57, 58, 62
Wolf River Rig, 91
Worms, 20, 107

Y
Yellow Bullhead, 40
See also: Bullheads

Creative Publishing international, Inc. offers a variety of how-to books. For information write:
Creative Publishing international, Inc.
Subscriber Books
5900 Green Oak Drive
Minnetonka, MN 55343

-Editor's Note-

The author, Keith Sutton, is Editor of *Arkansas Wildlife* magazine, a conservation publication of the Arkansas Game & Fish Commission, and a Field Editor for *In-Fisherman's Catfish In-Sider.* He also is a prolific freelance writer, photographer and lecturer, well known in his native South.

3 6058 00110 7289